Who Ever Heard of a
HORSE
in the
HOUSE?

Jacqueline Tresl

J. N. TOWNSEND PUBLISHING
EXETER, NEW HAMPSHIRE
2000

Jacket design by Design Point.

Printed in Canada.

Published by
J. N. Townsend Publishing
12 Greenleaf Drive
Exeter, New Hampshire 03833
1-800-333-9883
www.jntownsendpublishing.com

Library of Congress Cataloging-in-Publication Data
Tresl, Jacqueline.
Who ever heard of a horse in the house?/ Jacqueline Tresl.
p. cm.

ISBN: 1-880158-27-2
1. Horses--Anecdotes. 2. Women horse owners--Anecdotes. 3. Tresl, Jacqueline. I. Title.

SF301.T74 2000
636.1'0887--dc21   99-088852

To Momma, Mark and Misha, and the redemptive power of their unconditional love.

Who ever heard of a horse in the house?
Shouldn't she be in a barn?
Of course, I have my mouse in the house,
But who ever heard of a horse in the house?

Richard Meibers

Chapter One

I never planned to have a house-horse. I didn't even know it could be done. The idea of sharing my living room with my foal sneaked up on me. But her boundless devotion to me overcame any hesitation I might have had. Instead of dismissing it as an outrageous idea, I wound up saying, "She wants to be with me and I want to be with her, so why not bring my foal inside?"

Turned out it wasn't hard to do. But the day-to-day routine of sharing a small living space with a horse was something altogether different. Imagine living with a 1,400-pound perpetually hungry two-year-old toddler. Everything you leave out on the counter or on the floor goes into her mouth. Any electrical wires or phone cords have to be out of her reach. Never again can you eat a meal without those big, gorgeous brown eyes watching and following every bite you spoon into your mouth.

Having a horse in the house is like having a gigantic, undereducated, mulish preschooler who never grows up. She tracks mud in the house, so I have to vacuum every day. She drinks from the bathtub while I am bathing. She doesn't understand that she should use a handkerchief. Some days I want to pull out my hair, but most of the time, I can't believe how lucky I am. My horse is my shadow since I brought her inside.

If I leave the room, she follows me. If she can't find me, she nickers. If I go shopping, she gets sweaty and anxious and positions herself like a sentry or a statue at the driveway gate until I get home. She adores me fiercely, and in her eyes I can do no wrong. She makes me feel like the most special woman in the world.

Our love affair began thirteen years ago. Before we met, I had spent two years "shopping" for my perfect, first horse. I'd seen them all: thoroughbreds, Arabians, paints, and mixed-up breeds. Pedigree wasn't important to me, nor was color, size, or gender. I was looking for a horse with a built-in love of life and a sparkling, inquisitive personality. None of the horses I saw for sale had that certain *je ne sais quoi*. I had almost given up hope. Then one day at work, a nurse told me a sad tale about her sister Helen. After twenty-six years of marriage, Helen suddenly found herself abandoned when her husband fell in love with a younger woman. Helen was left as the sole caretaker for her husband's thirty-one registered quarter horses.

My friend said, "Poor Helen doesn't know what she's going to do. She has six weanlings that aren't even off their mothers yet. She doesn't have enough hay for the winter, the stalls need mucked and her husband left her $100 in their bank account to live on."

I drove by Helen's that evening after work. She looked thin, shaky, and grossly overworked. I asked her if she had any horses to sell. She pointed towards the barn and said, "Take your pick," then left me and hustled back inside her house.

The barn was a horror. The stalls were filled with manure three feet deep. The horses could barely lift their legs to move because the manure was up to their knees. They looked dull, hungry, and war torn. Tears welled up in my eyes.

I told myself I should get out of there, that this awful scene would replay itself over and over in my mind and I'd be tortured with nightmares. But when I started to leave, over in the corner in one of the bigger stalls, a tiny sorrel foal with a swirl of white on her head slogged her way through the manure to look me right in the eye. As soon as I looked back at her, she tossed her head and nickered.

I walked away. The foal kept staring at me. When I said goodbye to the last horse in the barn, the foal whinnied. When I came back over to her, she nickered and winked. I knew then I had found my horse and my horse had found me.

Helen agreed to sell the foal. And because she was in dire financial straits and I didn't have much money, she said she'd give me a bargain—my registered quarter horse baby for $360 plus forty hours of pitchforking manure out of the stalls.

My husband, Mark, came back with me the next day. He did most of the mucking. I couldn't concentrate on anything but my foal. I brought her carrots and corn on the cob, cooed to her and petted her. Somehow I ignored the green pus dripping from her nostrils and the yellow goop encrusted around her eyes. I noticed that her ribs poked out, her hooves smelled rank, and her breathing was often labored. But none of it mattered because I was in love.

My husband asked me if our foal was sick. I said, "So what if she is. Does it matter? We love her and she's ours. Healthy or not, she's coming to live with us."

For three days, we mucked stalls while admiring and fussing over our foal. We decided to name her Misha, which is a Russian word for "little mouse." Back then, to us, she seemed small and timid.

At the end of the week, we paid a man with a truck and trailer to bring Misha home to us. Trouble was, she had never been handled. She'd never worn a halter or been separated from her mother. When her stall door opened, she panicked and froze. There was no coaxing her out.

So Helen led Misha's mother into our borrowed trailer and Misha followed right behind. Then Helen walked the mother back out and Mark shut the trailer door before Misha could bolt out.

My husband rode in the back of the trailer with her. It was a cold and windy October afternoon. Misha's fur was thin and horribly matted. I was following behind the trailer in our VW Bug and I watched Mark take off his heavy wool jacket and lay it across Misha's back. I worried that he'd catch pneumonia. Right before we got home, he slipped a foal-sized green halter over Misha's head.

Our house and barn are down in a wooded hollow. Our driveway is eight hundred feet long, and steep. The man driving the truck and trailer refused to come all the way down our driveway. Instead, he stopped halfway and parked on a level spot.

The stall we'd readied for Misha was a ten-foot-square log house located four hundred feet away from where the man parked his truck. When we opened the trailer door, Misha refused to come out. She pushed herself up into the darkest, farthest corner and shivered. Mark tried to coax her out by pulling on her lead. She wouldn't budge. He and I pushed on her from behind. She was wedged in and wouldn't move. Finally, remembering how thin and starved she was, I said, "How about we try to lead her out with some corn?"

I laid a pile of corn at the edge of the trailer and another pile on the ground right below the trailer. Mark and I waited outside, a few feet away, with the lead pulled taut on her halter. Ten minutes later, Misha eased up to the first pile and began munching.

She moved her front feet down out of the trailer onto the ground, and ate the second pile. She kept her back feet in the trailer with her butt sticking up in the air. I laid down another pile, a little farther out. But as she leaned forward to get the corn, her back feet slipped out of the trailer. When her feet hit the ground, she leapt straight up in the air as if we'd stuck a sharp knife in her belly. Then she dragged Mark (who never let go of the lead) back and forth across the driveway a few times and ran around to the front of the truck.

The owner of the truck and trailer chuckled and said, "Well, I'll leave you two on your own now. My missus is waiting my supper." He tipped the bill of his cap, revved up his engine and left.

How hard could it be to get this sickly foal down our driveway and into her stall? We assumed that when we tugged on her lead, she would walk. We assumed wrong. She was immobilized by terror. Misha weighed about 400 pounds then. My husband is 6 feet tall and very strong. But that evening, he met his match.

The sun was setting and it was getting cold. "We have to get Misha into her stall," I insisted.

"You think I don't know that?" Mark answered, exasperated.

"What are we going to do?" I asked.

"The only thing we can do. I'll have to drag her."

"But she weighs twice as much as you," I pointed out.

"Well, do you have any better ideas?" Mark asked.

I didn't. Mark kept a steady pressure on Misha's lead and I moved her feet. While he tugged, I bent down and pried one of her hooves off the ground to move it forward a few steps. Sometimes Mark could catch her off balance while I was manipulating her feet and yank her a couple of yards down the driveway.

It was slow going. I could only lift up one foot at a time. Exactly 93 minutes later and in nearly pitch black, we finally got her to the doorway of her stall. Then she refused to take the one step up so she could walk into it. We got her head positioned over the threshold, levered both her front feet into the stall, and on the count of three, we gave one gigantic push against her behind. At last, she was inside her stall.

I cried. Mark folded up in a heap. Misha looked around at her new home and her muscles relaxed. She sniffed at her stall floor covered with three feet of fresh straw, sniffed at her mineral block and self-watering bowl and her manger filled with pure alfalfa hay.

Mark wanted some supper and a bath, so he left Misha and me alone inside the stall. Those first hours she and I spent together were magical. I crouched in a corner and watched her eat. I witnessed the true meaning of the word "starved."

She ate every blade of hay in her manger and tore off and chewed big chunks from the mineral block. I filled her grain bucket with sweet feed and she devoured it. I was afraid to give her too much more.

After an hour, she lay down in her stall, resting her head against my leg. She sighed and fell asleep. Her eyes rolled back in her head and the whites of her eyeballs twitched and jerked. I think it was the best sleep she'd ever had; for the first time in her five months of life she had gone to bed with a full stomach.

Sometime after midnight, Mark came out to check on us. He sat beside me and together we listened to Misha's soft snoring. We breathed in her delicious horse smell. Around two A.M. she stood up, stuck her nose into her hay manger and peered over at us. Mark got her another big flake of alfalfa hay.

I said, "I'm the luckiest woman in the world. Good night, Misha." With that, my husband and I ended our first official day with our new horse. Once inside the house, we collapsed onto our bed.

I woke up early and didn't bother getting dressed. I had to see for myself—did I really have a soft, sweet foal waiting for me in the little log house? I grabbed a handful of Chips Ahoy cookies and rushed out to the stall.

As soon as I pushed open her door, Misha nickered long and loud. She bumped her nose under my armpit. I couldn't believe my eyes—she was right where I'd left her, safe and happy and all mine. She gobbled down the chocolate chip cookies, sighed, and flopped back down in the straw.

I sat down with her. The birds were whistling their early morning songs. My husband stuck his head out the kitchen door and yelled, "Hon? Hon? What's for breakfast?" I was torn. If I got up and left the stall, I'd disturb Misha's nap. If I stayed in the stall, my husband would be hungry.

I eased my way out and went into the house. A few minutes

later, I tiptoed back and peeked through the stall window. Misha was flat out, her hooves running in her sleep.

For the next three hours I kept checking. She kept sleeping. I said to Mark, "Boy, she must really be tired."

He said, "Imagine how you'd feel if you'd lived with manure up to your knees and had a mother who was too starved to be able to make enough milk to feed you. If I were Misha, I'd sleep all day, too."

My husband left for work. I did three loads of laundry, made bread, and vacuumed out the car. Misha was still asleep. I made a sandwich and took it and a lawn chair into the stall and sat with her. An hour later, she got up.

She yawned, then coughed and coughed and coughed. Green mucus dripped from her nose and yellowish tears rolled down from her eyes. The sight of all that pus scared me.

I thought about leaving her to call the vet, but when I tried to get up, she sank her nose into my lap. She was asking me to stay with her. So I settled back in.

I was still in the stall at six o'clock when Mark got home. He brought Misha a big flake of hay while I got her a scoop of feed. She coughed while she ate, but she acted happy.

Finally, I went in to make our own dinner. It was after eight before Mark had his meal. As we settled in for the evening, I said, "Honey, Misha's awfully sick. What am I going to do?"

"What can you do?" he sighed. "Just try your best."

The next morning I drove to the feed store and bought two tubes of worming medicine and a big bottle of penicillin. As soon as I got home, I estimated Misha's weight and dosed her for worms, then drew up five ccs of penicillin and injected it into her neck.

As a nurse, I've administered many shots before, but never to a horse. It took me three attempts to puncture through her thick muscle. As soon as the needle was in, she took off, running around in circles. Every time I got close enough to pull the needle out from her neck, she ran away from me.

Finally, I cornered her and removed the syringe. She was out of breath and sweating. "Good girl," I said. "You'll be okay." I gave her an apple and sat with her.

The stress was too much and within minutes, she started to cough. After five minutes of her rasping snorts, I had to leave. I hated to hear her suffering.

An hour later Misha's breathing settled down, and she was hungry. She instantly wolfed down every bite of food I gave her. A half a bale of hay later, she was still hungry.

I went out to get her some sweet feed. When I came back in, I gasped. In front of her doorway was a pile of manure, and at least half of it was long white spaghetti.

"Oh my God, Misha," I cried. "What's happened to you? Are those pieces of your intestine?"

She was too concerned about her feed to pay me any attention. I poured the grain into her bucket and spotted a second pile. I put on my work gloves, carried the "spaghetti" out into the sunlight and realized it wasn't pasta or pieces of her gut—it was worms. Long, ugly, energy-zapping roundworms. I dug deeper and found threadworms, pinworms, and bots. No wonder her stomach was so swollen and she was always so starved. She was feeding an army of parasites.

Later that day, I dosed her with more penicillin and fed her lots of hay. The next morning she was coughing less and eating a little bit slower, less ravenously. But she needed some exercise, sunshine, and green grass. She hadn't left her stall since that first evening out of the trailer.

Mark was skeptical about my taking her out. "What if she gets loose? Are you going to be able to drag her back into the stall? Wait until the weekend when I'm home. She can stay in the stall till then."

I didn't want her to have to wait. She was fragile and sickly and I was convinced she'd feel better if she got some fresh air. So that morning, I started training her in her stall.

"Walk, Misha," I'd say, while tugging on her lead. "Whoa,

Misha," and I'd hold her back. Within minutes she was walking and stopping on command. I was proud of her and rewarded her with carrots.

Throughout the day, I returned to the stall and repeated the lesson. Every time I asked her to walk, she moved forward without delay. Each time I asked her to whoa, she came to an abrupt stop. "What a smart girl you are," I said.

Just before Mark was due home from work, I led Misha out of her stall on halter and lead. I asked her to walk with me to the driveway and stop at the gravel. She did. Then she dug her face into the tall grass and clover and ate furiously.

Mark pulled in from work, saw us and shook his head. He rolled down his window and said, "You know you took an unnecessary risk."

But after a while of watching Misha gobble her grass as the evening sun set behind her shoulders, he said, "You two did good. I'm proud of my girls."

Misha didn't want to go back in her stall, but I needed to make Mark's supper. Our yard wasn't fenced in, so I couldn't just let her run loose. I said, "Misha, it's time to go back to your stall." She ignored me and kept eating.

I said, "C'mon, good girl, walk for me."

She lifted up her head. Grass was dangling from the sides of her mouth. She looked deeply into my eyes, then followed right beside me till we got to her stall door. I went inside the stall first and asked her to walk. She marched right in. I took off her halter and poured her some sweet feed. Even though she was busy eating, she nickered when I closed her stall door.

Three hours later I checked on her. She was lying flat out in her stall. Her breathing was slow and easy and her stomach looked a little less puffed. Her nose wiggled and her ears twitched while she dreamed of fields filled with clover and of her new and better life. Misha had learned a lot since coming to live with us, and now her dreams were sweet.

Chapter Two

No matter how much green grass I gave Misha, it was never enough. A wheelbarrow full of tall, lush timothy would last her ten minutes; a sack of fresh white clover was nothing more than a small snack. Even though I filled her up with sweet feed and alfalfa hay, Misha craved grass.

We had no fenced-in pasture. Our twenty acres were open to the dirt road and our neighbor's field, so I couldn't let Misha out of her stall to graze unless I was with her. For a few weeks, I tried to cut enough grass for her to eat while she was in her stall, but I could never keep up with her demand. Some days I'd have to walk a half mile of roadside to fill my sack. And even then, after I'd collected grass for an hour, it barely made a dent in her empty stomach.

Fence building became a priority. I asked Mark if he thought he could find a little bit of extra time to start on her fence.

"A little bit of time?" he asked, incredulous. "Jackie, building fence takes a whole lot of time and is awfully hard work. You think 'a little bit of time' is all it'll take?"

"Well, maybe not, but Misha's starved for grass. And I hate to see her suffer."

"Yeah, yeah, yeah. I'll build your fence but you'll have to wait a couple of weeks till I get my other chores done. Can you make out all right till then?"

"Oh thank you, honey!" I hugged him. "Yes, we'll make out just fine till you can get to it."

So while we waited for our fence, Misha and I spent most of our days grazing together in the field. After leading her out of her stall to a juicy patch of grass, I'd sit on the ground beside her, prop open a book and keep an eye on her while I read. I attached one end of a fifty-foot clothesline to her halter and wrapped the other end around my wrist, figuring if she tried to run away, she'd have to drag me with her. But she never did. In fact, I had the opposite problem. She tried to stand almost on top of me.

No matter where I was sitting, Misha thought the best-tasting grass was the grass around my legs and feet or, if I was lying down, the grass around my shoulders and head. If I moved out of her way, she followed me and switched to the next patch of grass surrounding me. She loved to graze with her nose pressed against my thigh or my shoe.

After a while, I didn't bother with the clothesline because Misha never tried to run away or get onto the road. As long as I was sitting next to her in the grass, she stayed right beside me. I got more reading done in those two months than I had in the past three years.

As soon as I bought Misha, I read all the horse books that our library had. When I finished those, I ordered more through the interlibrary loan system. Before Misha was nine months old, I'd read eighty-three books about horse training, equine anatomy, behavior, and communication.

Trouble was, my housework began to suffer because I was always outside grazing with Misha. Dust balls were growing under my furniture, and my floors felt kind of sticky. I had to find a way Misha could be outside her stall without me so I could get my work done.

I was at wit's end until I had the bright idea to stick her in my 200' x 200' fenced-in garden, which had grass around the sides and lots of dandelions and Queen Anne's lace growing in the middle. Every day, after her breakfast and a good thorough brushing, I'd put Misha in the garden while I rushed back to do my morning house chores, hustling around to get the bed made, the dishes washed and the floors mopped. Because we live in the woods, my garden is set six hundred feet away from our house so it can get the full sun. That meant while Misha was in the garden, I couldn't see her and she couldn't see me. But I could hear her.

If I left her alone in the garden for more than an hour, she'd get restless, stop nibbling, and start nickering for me. If, after an hour and a half, I still didn't come get her, she'd start whinnying and galloping around in small circles.

One day I was determined to make her stay in the garden long enough so that I could get all my walls washed down. It was two hours before I finished, and I'd heard her calling for me the whole last hour. By the time I got my rubber gloves off, dumped my pail, and set off to retrieve her, she was soaked with sweat and couldn't stop coughing because she'd overexerted herself from running around the garden so long.

After that episode, I limited myself to an hour of morning chores. Once they were finished, I spent almost every afternoon grazing with her. By now, it was November and even when the sun was out, I got pretty cold. But Misha yearned for the fresh grass and she couldn't seem to settle without me right beside her.

Meanwhile, Mark was cutting and gathering locust fence posts and digging postholes. He was also lugging home a winter's supply of alfalfa hay and straw bedding. He told me he thought he'd have the fence up by the end of December. "But," he said, "you can't keep sitting outside with Misha till then."

"I'll sit out with her as long as I can stand it. Besides, we're bonding and I'm getting a lot of reading done."

What Misha hated most were the three evenings a week I left

her to go to my job as an ICU nurse. Whenever I knew I'd have to work, I'd spend all morning and early afternoon with her because once I left for the hospital, she had to stay in her stall until I got home.

Mark would check on her several times while I was gone, but he almost never took her outside to graze. By the time I'd get home at midnight, Misha was almost crazed from loneliness and abandonment. Many nights, as soon as I changed out of my uniform, I took Misha out to graze until 2 or 3 A.M.. I always wore my thickest winter coat and took along a heavy blanket. Exhausted after caring for critically ill patients all evening, I rolled myself up in the blanket to watch the twinkling stars and often fell asleep to the sound of Misha chewing not five paces from my head.

Mark didn't like my sleeping out in the cold grass after I'd just gotten home from working eight hours. He said he was ready to start building the fence and that whenever he worked on it and I wasn't home, he'd take Misha along with him. "She can graze as we go and watch me put in every fence post."

"But what if she tries to wander?" I worried.

"I'll tie her to something that I can move along with me as I work." He thought a minute. "I'll use a tire. I'll tie her to a tire and move it from post to post."

So on the weekends when I went to work, the last thing I saw as I drove out my dirt road was Misha clotheslined to a tire, grazing beside Mark while he dug holes and set posts. Usually he worked till dark, so Misha got to graze for three or four hours. She was still excited to see me when I got home at night, but after "helping" to build fence, she was so full and tired she didn't need me to take her outside. It was such a treat to come home, sit in the stall, visit with her, and then be able to jump into my soft bed.

One Sunday when Mark and Misha were out building fence, our next-door neighbor stopped by and asked Mark to help him pull his truck out of the mud. Mark asked, "Will it take very long? Because if it does, I'll have to put the horse in her stall."

"Oh no, it'll be quick. If you'll steer the truck, I can pull it out with my tractor in a minute," the neighbor said.

Misha was grazing and didn't seem to be paying attention to Mark or the neighbor. Mark made sure Misha was tied securely to the tire and told her to wait there—he'd be right back. He walked across the yard over to the neighbor's and was just sliding himself into the neighbor's truck when he heard thundering hooves and a constant "thud, thud, thud." He looked up and saw Misha galloping across our field over to the neighbor's, dragging the bouncing tire behind her. As soon as she found Mark, she settled in beside him and, still attached to her tire, calmly started to graze.

Mark had Misha's fence finished two weeks before Christmas. Now she could run free and graze unsupervised. At first, she was delighted. I'd let her out of her stall early in the morning and she'd frolic and nibble her way through the cold dewy grass. But after an hour, she'd wander back over to the house and call to me, nickering with great gusto. If nickering didn't bring me out, she'd whinny shrilly. And if I still didn't come out, she'd prance in circles around the house, stopping occasionally to peer in the windows.

As soon as she'd spot me in the living room or kitchen, she'd nicker and bang her nose back and forth across the glass. Until I came outside, she stood vigil around the house while periodically "knocking" on the various windows.

Most days I'd stop what I was doing to go out and sit in the field with her while she grazed. But since it was late December, my fingertips would feel numb after a few minutes. As soon as I tried to head back to the house, Misha followed me. She didn't want to graze if I wasn't going to graze with her.

I tried all sorts of ways to stay warm while I sat outside with her. I heated my boots up so hot I could barely slip my feet into them without getting burned. I took out quart-sized steaming mugs of tea to drink while she grazed. I layered sweaters, socks, gloves, and hats, but by the time Christmas rolled around, I was always pretty cold. As soon as I headed back inside, Misha followed me to the house.

She stood guard outside our windows for three days before Mark said, "Why did you have me rush around and build a fence if your horse is going to hang around outside the house all the time? Why don't you push her out into the field?"

"I've tried, but she wants to be close to me. I'm hoping if I ignore her, she'll outgrow it," I said.

That evening at dinner, Misha played sentry outside the kitchen window and watched us eat. Then she whinnied. "Don't pay her any attention," Mark said.

Five minutes later we heard a "bamm" and a "thunk," followed by another and another. We ran to the window and watched Misha lift up her front hoof and smack it against the windowsill over and over again.

I went outside. She was shivering and anxious. She still had not completely recovered from her foal pneumonia; her nose was dripping and her breathing was labored.

I hugged her and cooed. She stopped shivering and threw her head over my shoulder. "What's the matter?" I asked.

I stayed outside to calm her. My supper was ruined. Every time I tried to go back inside, Misha tagged behind me. As soon as I'd open the kitchen door, she'd wail long and loud. As soon as I'd shut the door and come back out to her, she'd press herself against me.

I called to Mark. "Misha is suffering from acute separation anxiety."

He said, "So what are you going to do about it? Live outside with her?"

"Well, no. Ah, actually, I thought maybe I'd bring her inside with me for a little while."

21

"What? Are you nuts? She's a horse. She can't come inside," he said.

"Why not? She doesn't weigh much more than a really big dog and as soon as she feels the warmth of the woodstove and has me in her sight, she'll settle right down and fall asleep. She won't be any trouble, I promise."

Mark looked at me, shook his head, and sighed.

"Oh please, honey, just for the winter. I promise I'll make her stay outside as soon as spring comes. But look at her...she's so cold and sickly and lonely and..."

"Enough already. Okay, all right, bring her in and quit whining. You two are a couple of nuts," he said.

He went to the barn and got a rug to lay across the kitchen linoleum. I put a halter and lead on Misha and opened the back door as wide as it would go. Mark said, "How is she ever going to walk up that one high step to get into the house?"

I said, "You watch. She'll follow me anywhere."

I pulled gently on her lead and said, "C'mon, good girl, wanna come in the house with me?"

She looked me in the eye, took a deep breath, lined herself up with the step and in under thirty seconds was standing beside my refrigerator, our very biggest, thickest throw rug under her feet.

Chapter Three

I f horses smile, then Misha was grinning from ear to ear the second she stepped into my kitchen. Her ears perked up and she seemed to say, "Now this is where I was always meant to be."

The woodstove was blazing hot and stew was simmering. Misha stood perfectly still for a moment, enraptured by the sudden warmth of the house and intoxicated by the smell of food cooking. She sniffed the countertops, the rug, the dish towels and pot holders; then she eased up as close as she could get to the woodstove without singeing her hair and within minutes, was swaying on her feet, fast asleep.

I rewarmed my dinner, curled up in my chair and watched Misha snooze. I could smell her fur getting hot from the stove. Her head was nearly touching the chimney, and when I put my hand out to feel her cheek, her skin felt like it was on fire.

"Don't you think maybe you should move away from the stove, Misha?" But when I tried to pry her away, she wouldn't budge. She leaned back over against the stove and continued to sleep.

She never moved for the next three hours. It was as if this was the first time in her whole life she'd ever been thoroughly warm. I washed the dishes around her while opera music boomed out over the speakers. Mark rehung a shelf ten feet away from her head. Nothing we did bothered her as long as she was by the stove.

Then all of a sudden she woke up and was restless. She shifted her weight and fussed with the firewood, the rug edge, and the light switch. She turned around and walked over to the kitchen door, looked back at me, and pawed.

"Something's wrong with Misha," I said to Mark.

"Yes, you've probably boiled her internal organs."

"No, really, honey, something's wrong," I said.

Just then, it hit me; she probably needed to relieve herself. I opened the kitchen door to let her out, but she wouldn't go. When I walked up to her head, she nudged me.

"What? You want me to go out with you? But it's dark and cold," I said.

She didn't move. Then she pawed again. I got my coat and went outside. She followed right behind me, walked 100 feet from the house, did her business, nudged me, and headed back.

I opened the kitchen door and let her inside. I told Mark, "This horse is so smart. You want to know why she was so restless? She had to do her business and she didn't want to do it in the house."

"She better not do it in the house or she's never coming inside again," he said.

"Yes, but do you understand what I'm trying to tell you? She knew that she needed to go outside. Do you know what this means? It means maybe she can be housebroken."

"Why would you want to housebreak her? She has a stall and a 20-acre fenced-in lot, remember? Nobody said anything about her living in the house."

"Well, I was thinking. She's still sickly and obviously she's cold. Plus she hates to be outside by herself. It's almost January and I can't spend the winter outside with her, so how about if we let her spend part of each day in the house with us, just until spring."

"Are you crazy?" Mark asked. "She's a horse. She'll break the floor, she'll knock stuff over, we won't have any room in the kitchen to move around."

Mark is a softie. He tries to act tough, but deep down he's as gentle as any macho alpha male can be. It didn't take me long to convince him that Misha should spend the winter in our kitchen.

"But," he said, "promise me it's temporary, only until the spring, when she's healthier and it's warm outside."

"Oh thank you, honey. Yes, I promise. Just for the winter." I gave him a big kiss and hugged Misha.

Life got easier for me as soon as Misha began spending her days in the house. Every morning before making Mark's breakfast, I'd go outside and let Misha out of her stall. We'd walk over to the house together and she'd follow me into the kitchen to "help" whisk omelets or mix up pancake batter. As soon as Mark ate his breakfast and left for work, I'd tie a loose line from Misha's halter to my refrigerator door handle. That way I could do my morning chores without worrying about her wandering around the house when I wasn't paying attention.

But I shouldn't have bothered. By the time Mark was done eating, she would have worn herself out after begging through his entire meal. As soon as I'd start washing the dishes, she'd wedge herself up close to the woodstove and sleep. I could vacuum around her hooves, dust over her head, wax the linoleum under her nose and she'd never wake up. As long as she was near me, she was relaxed.

But since her lungs had been compromised from early foal pneumonia, dust from the woodstove would sometimes trigger a coughing spell. One morning I was sweeping up the ash from under the stove, and some dust must have floated into her lungs. She coughed so violently I was worried she'd choke. I walked her outside to get her away from the dust, but an hour later she was still coughing and spitting up phlegm. I was scared because I didn't know how to make her stop.

I had talked to my veterinarian many times about Misha's pneumonia and her chronic cough. He had no miraculous cures up his sleeve. He felt I was probably exaggerating her symptoms because, he said, "If she coughed as much as you say she does, she'd be a whole lot sicker than she is."

So, not knowing what else to do, I walked her around outside to move the fresh air in and out of her lungs. I gave her a boxful of cough drops to chew and a freezer pop to soothe her throat. All of it helped her a little bit, but still, she continued to cough.

Finally, I filled a pail with icy cold water and added a package of Kool-Aid drink mix. I offered the sweet drink to Misha and she gulped it down. As soon as the pail was empty, she lifted her head and sighed. Miraculously, her coughing jag had ended.

But most days she didn't cough much and spent her mornings sleeping by the stove until my work was done. Then we'd go outside together to graze. Sometimes she'd let me leave her and I'd use the opportunity to sneak off to town for groceries and fresh library books. But most of the time, she kept her eyes on me and if I headed back to the house and stayed too long, she'd be at the kitchen door, pawing to be let in.

By 3 P.M., she always settled herself in the house for the rest of the day. She loved to supervise supper-making. If I peeled a pound of carrots for vegetable soup, I gave her the ends and the peels to eat. If I kneaded bread, I gave her a lump of unbaked dough. If I made oatmeal cookies, I handed her a heap of raisins and uncooked oats.

Her first winter in the kitchen was her equine kindergarten. It's where and when I started to teach her discipline, manners, language, and the concept of trust. I taught her to wait until I offered her tidbits and treats; she was never allowed to reach over onto the counter and grab them. She couldn't stick her tongue into unwashed baking bowls until I invited her. And she learned not to knock the dishes around when they were drying on the dish rack.

26

By the age of eight months, she understood the meaning of "hot" after she tried to eat freshly boiled brussels sprouts. She learned how important it was to keep her face off of my cutting board when my paring knife accidentally nicked her lip.

Some days we had minor tussles. Even as small as she was, she was still a lot bigger than I. Her head was powerful and her reflexes quick. She could steal a peeled potato out from under my nose so fast she'd have most of it eaten before I could grab it back. Once in a while, she'd push me too far and have to be punished.

To Misha, the most horrible punishment in the world is when I ignore her. Second on her list is when I withhold her treats. So if she fussed over the cookie sheet too much or bumped too many of my clean dishes around, I made her stand outside for ten minutes. If she snatched food off platters or stuck her nose into simmering pots, I refused to give her any snacks. But if she behaved herself and wasn't a nuisance while I prepared dinner, I offered her little treats of food the entire time I cooked.

One Friday Mark was late getting home from work. As soon as Misha heard him pull down the driveway, she whinnied and pawed. She couldn't wait for him to walk through the door and sit down at the table because she was hyperexcited about supper. We were having one of her all-time favorites—spaghetti. She turned around in circles to greet him when he came in and as she shifted back around to point him to the table, her head swung over the pot. Two pounds of cooked spaghetti and sauce landed on the floor.

A few months later, Mark and I were playing Monopoly while Misha stood by the electric stove, guarding the peanut butter cookies as they baked. She kept resting her nose against the oven door gasket so she could smell the cookies. I had her loosely tied to the refrigerator door so that she wouldn't saunter over to the Monopoly board and try to eat the pieces. Just before the cookies were done, Misha decided her chin itched. She tried to use the oven door handle as a scratching post and when she did, the ring of her halter caught on the side of the door handle. As soon as she yanked her head away, the halter ripped the oven door off its hinges. The door flew up over her head, smacked against the porcelain kitchen countertop, and jackknifed into a cabinet.

Misha's eyes got so huge the whites showed. She was scared by the catapulting oven door but was more scared, I think, that we'd be angry with her.

I scratched under her mane and talked softly until she was calm. Mark came over to assess the damage. The oven door was twisted, the handle was bent and one of the oven hinges was ripped out and hanging. I said, "Well, at least Misha wasn't hurt."

Mark protested, "What about me? This will take me hours to repair."

I moved Misha away from the kitchen and onto the living room rug. We both watched while Mark fixed the oven door. He pried and hammered, drilled and tapped. An hour later, my oven was as good as new.

Considering her size, Misha was never much trouble when she was in the house. Mostly she slept, except around mealtime when she mooched and begged for food.

About every three hours, I slipped a halter and lead on her and took her outside to do her business. I couldn't count on her to always tell me when she needed to go. I didn't ever want her to have an accident in the house because I figured once she had urinated or defecated on the floor, she might be tempted to think it was an acceptable practice. So I tried to put her bladder and bowels on a rigid schedule. I never let her stay in the house longer than four hours without taking her out.

Many times the winds were howling and the snows were blowing. I'd be in my nightie, snuggled up cozy by the fire. Then it would be time to take Misha out and I'd have to pull on my parka, hat, and boots, and face the harsh winter night. Usually Misha did her business quickly, but sometimes she wanted to push around the snow or itch against a tree or fiddle with a low-hanging branch and I'd be out with her a whole lot longer than I wanted. But it's hard to hurry a horse.

At bedtime, Misha had to sleep in her stall. There wasn't enough room for her to lie down in the kitchen and I didn't want to have to wake up two times a night to take her out for her business. She always balked when it was bedtime. She hated to leave the warm house and played every trick on me she knew to postpone being put in her stall.

She'd nuzzle me, lick me, and toss her head to get me laughing. She knew if I was busy laughing at her, I'd be slower putting her to bed. Or she'd pretend to have an itch and waste five minutes scratching it. Or she'd find a minuscule bread crumb or dry noodle and fuss with licking, chewing, and swallowing. She had more ways to put off going to bed than a five-year-old.

I was always worried about putting her in the cold stall after she'd been in the warm house most of the day. I kept the stall door and window closed tight, but sometimes the temperatures at night dropped to ten degrees below zero. I expressed my concern to Mark and he said, "Oh, she'll be fine. You worry too much."

But she was sickly, skinny, and perpetually cold. I thought about buying her a blanket, but they cost $100 and since she'd have outgrown it by next winter, it seemed a terrible waste of money. Mark saw me looking at the expensive horse blankets in my catalogs and he said, "I could make you one of those a whole lot cheaper."

"You could? How?"

"I'd just take that wool Army blanket we have, cut it to Misha's size, sew on some straps, stitch the sides together and she'd be all set."

"Would you really do that?" I asked.

"Of course."

The next weekend, true to his word, Mark dug out his father's old duffel bag, found the Army blanket, and sewed Misha a warm winter coat. Every night when I put her to bed and strapped her new homemade horse coat around her belly, I felt like I was dressing her in a special pair of equine pajamas. I slept a lot better after that knowing she was warm.

During the coldest days of February, Misha stayed inside almost all day. One of the lessons she had to learn was how to be careful around my cat, Mouse.

Mouse was ten years old at the time and rapidly going deaf. He was a tiny kitten the day I rescued him from a dumpster in the hospital parking lot. When he was eight months old, I had him neutered. Twenty-four hours after his surgery, he had a grand mal seizure that lasted three minutes. Ten minutes later, he seized again. Within an hour he was in status epilepticus, a condition characterized by seizures that occur one right after another.

I rushed Mouse to my vet. He injected the cat with a hefty dose of Valium and I took Mouse home. The next day, his seizures resumed. For a week, Mouse was heavily medicated. Every time he resurfaced from his drugged daze, he cried and reached out for me to hold him. I spent hours and hours carrying him in my arms, his body limp from the Valium and the seizures.

The vet urged me to euthanize Mouse. But I loved him too much and was determined to find a better solution. I got a large, deep box and laid a thick blanket in the bottom. I put Mouse in the box and sat beside it, dangling my hand and my arm down into the box to rest on top of Mouse. For thirty-six hours I didn't let him out of the box. Even while I slept, I kept my hand on top of him.

I thought if I could limit Mouse's activity and all his external stimulation (light, sound, movement), his brain could rest and his nerves might settle down. At first, even in the box, he had a lot of seizures. But after a while, he had fewer. The next day, he only seized once. For Mouse, that box was his turning point. Within two days, I was able to let him out of the box so he could live a normal life again.

The vet and I decided to start him on a daily dose of phenobarbital. I crushed one pill and put it in his breakfast every day. Within a month, Mouse was seizure-free. But the status epilepticus had taken its toll. Mouse would always be weak. I never let him out of the house unless I was with him. Even though he always stayed in the yard, he was too delicate to be left unsupervised.

By the time Misha came to live with us, Mouse was losing his hearing. It took Misha a long time to understand that Mouse couldn't hear her when she approached him. Because Mouse had no peripheral vision, he would never see Misha until she was right on top of him. It was hard to teach Misha to look out for her "brother." She had to be responsible for keeping him safe when he got around her hooves.

I was having trouble teaching this lesson to her until the day Mark and I were working a jigsaw puzzle. Misha was sleeping next to us, her head hanging over the thousand pieces. I didn't see Mouse get off of his chair and curl up near my feet. A few minutes later, Misha shifted her weight and, without meaning to, she set her hoof down on Mouse's tail. He screamed in terror. Misha's eyes got big and she bolted out of the way. I picked Mouse up and snuggled him while Misha watched and listened. Then I made the most of the incident, using it as a lesson and a teaching tool.

I changed the tone in my voice so that Misha would know she'd done wrong. I carried Mouse over to her and repeated over and over, "You must be careful around your brother. You must always watch out for him." I put his mashed tail under her nose and let her smell where her hoof had come down on it. I told Mouse he was a good boy and I told Misha she had been "bad."

After that, Misha always looked down, checking under and around her feet when she was in the house. If Mouse came anywhere near her, she carefully watched where he was headed. If he sat down in front of her, she gently pushed him away with her nose.

I've read that horses will not deliberately hurt smaller animals. But Misha had to do more than not hurt him; she had to learn to protect him. And over the years, as Mouse lost his sight and his grand mal seizures returned, Misha would become his guardian angel.

Chapter Four

As early as February, Mark started to complain that Misha
had grown too big and too heavy to live in the house.
"One of these days your kitchen floor is going to collapse from all her weight and then you'll come crying, asking me to
fix it," he said.

He was right about how much she'd grown. We estimated that
she now weighed over 650 pounds. Our kitchen floor was made from
two-by-eights covered with a triple layer of half-inch plywood, and
was never designed to support a yearling horse. The floor sagged
gently all through the winter, but remained intact. Then came the
spring, the ticks, and our next domestic crisis, as the gentle sag in
the floor became a crater.

Spring of 1988 was rainy, warm, and a perfect incubating envi-
ronment for bugs. The tick population exploded. After an hour of
grazing in the tall, wet grass, Misha would amble back into the kitchen
with two dozen ticks climbing up her legs and tail.

Maybe because I brushed her every day or because she spent
most of her life inside a tidy house, Misha's skin was overly sensitive
to any little bits of dirt or tiny crawling things on her. She was greatly
annoyed whenever a tick tried to scoot up her leg and she couldn't
relax until she got rid of it. The only way she knew how to do that
was to stomp her hoof hard on the floor. Stomping made the tick

drop and fall onto the rug. But after a minute or two, the tick regained its equilibrium and climbed right back up Misha's leg again.

I spent many spring evenings on my hands and knees trying to root out all the ticks that tickled her. Sometimes I'd pick twenty or thirty off of her and assume that I'd gotten them all. But just as soon as I'd sit down in my chair, Misha would start stomping again. So back on my knees I'd go, searching for that last, elusive, offending tick. I had no choice. If I didn't, Misha might give one too many strong stomps and break through the kitchen floor. If that happened, Mark would be angry for sure.

Towards the end of March, one of the floor joists that supported the plywood finally did crack from her weight. I noticed the floor had cupped down as I walked between the stove and the sink. When I washed the linoleum, the water formed a puddle in the spot where Misha usually stood. I tried to hide that part of the floor from Mark by heaping a thick, textured throw rug over it, but he's hard to fool. He'd only been home from work for ten minutes before he noticed the bow. "What have I been telling you? Misha has destroyed the floor. That's it! She can't stand in the kitchen any more. It's too dangerous."

I whined and pleaded. Mark ignored my appeals. "Remember how you promised me that Misha would only be in the house for the winter? That you'd put her outside in the spring?"

I nodded and sniffled.

"Well, now the weather is warm. Misha is a lot healthier and the time has come for her to live where all other American horses live—outside!"

I didn't have a choice. A promise is a promise. I pushed Misha outside and locked the kitchen door. She cried and I cried. Mark told me to ignore her; our melodrama was tiresome. "If you'd stop acting sad, Misha could settle down to enjoying the grass and the sunshine."

I tried to cheer up, but my pretend smiles didn't help alleviate Misha's sorrow. She'd graze for twenty minutes, show up at the kitchen door, nicker, whinny, and rub her head against the doorknob. When I still didn't let her in, she'd mosey from windows to door, patrolling in search of me. As soon as she saw me through the glass, she'd wail and nudge the window. Mark still refused to let her back in.

Then Misha stopped grazing. She got diarrhea. She would only eat what I offered her from my hand. All day long she stood outside the kitchen door, head droopy, eyes listless, looking like an unloved orphan, never lying down to sleep, always on her legs, swaying, crying, heartbroken.

Eventually even Mark conceded we had to do something before Misha starved herself and fainted at our feet. He said he'd rethink Misha living in the house if we could come up with an acceptable compromise. He asked me if I had any ideas. I sprang Plan B on him.

"What's Plan B?" he asked.

"Well, first you shore up the kitchen floor. Then, while Misha waits in the kitchen, we'll build her a porch off the kitchen door. As soon as we get the porch finished, we'll make her spend the day out there so the kitchen floor doesn't cave in."

"We, huh? You're going to help me build a porch?"

"I'll do whatever I can to help. Besides, I've got the design all figured out in my head. Misha and I know exactly the kind of porch we want."

Mark spent one entire Saturday and most of Sunday crawling under the house to fix the cracked kitchen floor joist, sawing out old two-by-eights and replacing them with sections of steel I-beam. He told me the plywood had broken in several places, but without pulling off the kitchen linoleum, he had no way to repair the plywood from underneath. So he dug out two old car jacks from his junk pile and set them under the house. Then he jacked up the broken plywood until the kitchen floor was again somewhat level.

Sunday afternoon, Misha was back in the kitchen. She then

refused to leave the house, even to do her business. I think she was worried she'd never be allowed back in once she left. After six hours, I went outside with her. She fretted the whole time, inching towards the kitchen door even as she urinated, gratefully scrambling back in as soon as she was done. After a few days of this routine, Misha finally relaxed. She went back to grazing for a few hours and spending the rest of the day in the house.

It was around this time that she developed her lifelong passion for treats from Nickel's Bakery. Every time I left her to go to the hospital, I suffered enormous guilt. To alleviate my guilt, I often stopped at the Nickel's Thrift Bakery to buy Misha a sackful of day-old doughnuts, raspberry Danish, and sticky buns. As soon as I walked through the door at midnight (my ICU evening shift ended at 11:30 P.M.), I'd offer her the Nickel's bag and let her pick out a few packages of goodies. She even learned how to help me unwrap them. Jellyrolls and cream-filled doughnuts were her favorites.

There was one woman at the Thrift Bakery who always felt sorry for me, watching as I rushed around the store in my pristine white uniform trying to gather up a big bag of treats without being late for work. She would take pity on me, disappear into the back of the store, stuff thirty or forty packages of goodies into an old flour sack, haul out the enormous bag and hand it to me.

I'd ask, "How much?"

She'd say, "It's free."

My horse-owning friends had always berated me for giving Misha "junk food" because horses supposedly have delicate stomachs prone to colic. But Misha's doughnuts, cookies, and candy have never given her a bellyache. Misha has only had colic two times in her entire life, once after she'd eaten a Lodi apple, the second after grazing on frosted grass.

On days that I ran out of Nickel's baked goods, I substituted corn flakes, mashed potatoes, spaghetti (raw or cooked), peanut butter toast, and scrambled eggs. I was so glad to have Misha back inside the kitchen with me that I was guilty of overindulging her for a couple of months.

Meanwhile, Mark started excavation on the porch. He had to dig down through three feet of hard earth so he'd have enough room to pour the porch footings. Every evening until sunset, he shoveled dirt into a wheelbarrow and wheeled it away. I wanted the porch to be 12' x 12' so Misha would have plenty of room to lie down. Mark said that was too big and would only agree to build it 10 1/2' x 10 1/2'.

Mark was still worried about the kitchen floor even after he'd beefed it up with steel and jacks. Because of his concern, he worked at a fast and furious pace to get the porch done.

For two months, whenever he had even a spare half hour, he was pouring footings, cutting joists, laying plywood, and building log walls. He installed six windows and covered the floor with durable, thick rubber he salvaged from a coal-moving conveyor belt.

Mark made Misha's porch floor joists out of oak boards that were two inches thick and ten inches wide. He spaced the boards 10 inches apart. I thought that was a horrible waste of good, expensive wood. "I know she's heavy. But you act like she's an elephant," I said.

Mark disagreed. "Imagine how much force she will exert when she drops all her weight down on the porch to sleep. Plus, she's still a youngster. What about when she's full grown? You wait and see. You'll be glad these boards are big and spaced so close together," he said.

In May, two days after Misha's first birthday, her porch was done and she moved in. She loved the way the summer breezes and rays of sunshine drifted across her back without letting in any nasty blackflies to bite her. And since the porch was connected to the kitchen, Misha could still be close while I cooked meals and washed dishes.

Mark installed a hinged stick that acted as a skinny gate across the opening between her porch and the kitchen doorway. When I wanted to go out on her porch, rather than having to duck under the stick, Mark fixed it so that I could lift the stick up to walk through and put it back down when I was done. So while I baked and scrubbed, Misha kept her body on the porch and her head and neck hung over the stick, always keeping track of my movements.

But in the evenings, Misha was lonely because she was so far away from me, stuck out on her porch. After supper, I would scoot my chair up to within ten feet of her, but to a horse, that's not close enough. If you've ever watched a herd of sleepy horses, you'll see they are often touching each other, noses resting on each other's backs, standing head to rump or side to side. Misha would paw for me when I sat near her in the kitchen. According to her, I was sitting too far away.

After two weeks, I gave up, moved an old couch onto the porch and spent my evenings sitting out there with her. The minute I sat down on the couch, Misha would press some part of her body up against me. Our favorite evenings-on-the-porch position was my foot and lower leg tucked between her front leg and shoulder. As soon as I was settled in and she and I were touching, she would relax and sleep.

After many husbandless evenings on the porch, I started getting lonely for Mark. He liked to spend his evenings unwinding in front of the TV before bed. When I suggested he haul the TV out onto the porch and watch it there with us, he refused. Sometimes I'd ask him to come out and keep me company. He would, but within half an hour, he'd get fussy and bored or else fall asleep. Then I would have to whisper to Misha so I didn't wake him.

One evening Mark said he wasn't going to spend any more of his evenings out on the porch with me. "I built that porch so Misha would have some place to stand. I didn't build it for us to live in. That's why we have a house. Besides, there's nothing to do out there."

I had to get creative in a hurry and find a way to lure Mark back onto the porch. It was time for me to implement Plan C.

The next day was a Saturday, so I left Misha at home with Mark while I dashed over to the library. I browsed around the fiction shelves until I found three books on frontier life. Mark has always been a sucker for books about men and women in the eighteenth and nineteenth centuries who felled trees with handheld saws, cleared ground to plant gardens, and built pioneer communities while dangers lurked all around them. I initiated my Plan C with *Hannah Fowler*, a frontier novel by Janice Holt Giles.

Mark loves books, but because he's dyslexic, he's a painfully slow reader. Plan C was to read aloud to him. If I picked out books I knew he'd enjoy, I figured he'd follow me wherever I went with them, even if that meant out onto the porch.

Hannah Fowler was a great first book for us to share. Mark sat motionless and barely breathing while Hannah traveled to unsettled territories, hid from Indians, fought bears, married, and built a church. Mark was statue-still for hours as long as I was reading aloud. Misha stayed pressed up close against us.

That summer we read twenty-three books about the "old days." Our all-time favorite was an 896-page masterpiece called *The Peaceable Kingdom*. Some chapters I could barely get through. I cried so hard that I could hardly choke out the words. Misha licked my tears as I read aloud about little orphan children thrown into airless, dark dungeons, many of them waiting to be hanged.

As long as I was willing to read to Mark, he stayed out on Misha's porch with me. But then autumn came and the evenings were chilly. The woodstove in the center of our house wasn't big enough to adequately heat Misha's porch. By early October, my fingertips got so numb I had trouble flipping the pages. We hauled out huge mugs of hot cocoa and slipped on extra socks, but some evenings we couldn't get warm enough to feel comfortable.

Even though Misha had her own porch, she still couldn't spend the nights sleeping on it because she had no way of letting herself outside to do her business. And as it got colder, I worried that throwing Misha out into her stall every night might make her system susceptible to pneumonia.

After the first few heavy frosts, Mark pronounced it "too cold anymore to sit on the porch." He moved back into the living room and watched his new TV fall lineup. I stayed out on the porch with Misha a few more weeks before I also had to give up and come inside. The colder it got outside, the more difficult it was to keep the house warm. The porch was stealing too much of the woodstove's heat.

One especially cold afternoon, I couldn't seem to warm up, even with both the stove dampers wide open. I moved Misha back into the kitchen and closed the porch door. The house warmed right up to eighty degrees. Misha loved being able to help me make Mark's supper once again.

As soon as Mark got home from work, he scolded me for letting Misha back inside the house. "I'm warning you, that floor can't take her weight. You two are going to bust up this kitchen so bad I won't ever be able to fix it."

But since I know Mark can fix anything, it was an idle threat. I said, "Feel how warm it is in here now that Misha's back inside with us? Isn't it great? You don't want me to get sick because the house is so cold, do you?"

Mark didn't say much. He ate his supper and chuckled when Misha tossed her head over his pot roast and potatoes. He "accidentally" let some gravy and salad drop on the floor in front of her.

I said, "Isn't it wonderful how we're all back together again, just like the old days? Remember last winter when Misha stayed in the kitchen with us all the time?"

Mark nodded, wiped his mouth, and turned on the TV.

The next morning I couldn't find him. I searched his workshop and called until I was hoarse. Ten minutes later, he crawled out from under the kitchen, dead bugs and Owens Corning pink insulation stuck in his hair, mouse droppings on his clothes, and an industrial-sized drill in his hand.

"Where have you been?" I asked.

"Under the house."

"Well, I can see that. But why?"

"To re-reinforce the kitchen floor I reinforced last spring. If you two are bound and determined that Misha is going to spend the winter in the house, I want to make sure she doesn't fall through the floor."

"Oh, honey, does that mean you'll let her stay in the kitchen?"

"Do I have a choice? But it's only temporary, until we figure out something else to do with her."

Chapter Five

Tthere's a popular new pet pill out on the market. It's pre-scribed for animals that suffer with extreme separation anxiety.

Ten years ago, when I needed it, no such pill was available. Most veterinarians didn't even believe pets *had* anxiety. Until recently, I thought I was the only person in the world with an animal that went nuts every time I left her.

Misha hated it when I had to go to the ICU in the evenings. But she was only alone for two hours before Mark got home from work. Although he couldn't fill my "mother" shoes, he did provide a lot of company and comfort to her. She didn't like it when I went to the grocery store or the library, but I always kept my trips as short as possible. She would wait by the gate and graze until I got home. Then she'd nose around in my grocery sacks or book bags looking for treats.

The real trouble came when Mark and I wanted to go out to-gether. That triggered her acute separation anxiety. Mark and I loved playing tennis at the local college courts on our occasional free afternoons. On my weekends off, we enjoyed driving through Amish country searching for bargains, or spending a wintry evening cuddling at the movies. But after Misha's first birthday, that all ended. Mark and I stopped going out together.

As soon as Misha would hear the house keys jingle or see us putting on dressy clothes, she'd get restless, turn around in circles, knock things off the counter, and paw up her rug. We tried to ignore her. As soon as we put on our shoes and sweaters, she'd wail and block our way out of the door.

Trying to budge 800 pounds of twitching equine muscle is laborious. We were damp with sweat by the time we finally got her out of our way. But that was only our first hurdle. Once we had her out of the house and standing in the driveway, she'd dash over to the garage to block the doors. Then she'd block the car as Mark was trying to drive it out of the garage. When that still didn't keep us at home, she stood in front of the car as we tried to drive up the driveway. As soon as we got to the top of the driveway, she galloped to the gate and tried to sneak out while we opened it up. If we hadn't stopped her, she would have chased us, running behind our car, all the way to town just to be with us.

The situation was so desperate I didn't even bother getting into the car until it was out of the gate and on the dirt road. No matter if it was muddy, snowy, buggy, or rainy, I had to pry Misha out of the house, away from the garage doors, out from behind the car and in front of the car. Then some way or another, I had to get the gate opened and closed without letting her escape onto the road. Mark carried my good shoes out to the car while I chased Misha around in my waders or worn-out sneakers. As soon as we were on the road, I wiped the sweat off my brow and switched into decent shoes.

But that wasn't the worst of it. As soon as we drove away, Misha would start screaming as loud as she could. She'd gallop wildly in circles along the fence, head pointed in our direction, stopping every few minutes to let out another blood-curdling yell. It upset me so much I was wringing my hands before we'd gone a half mile. Mark would tell me to quit worrying. "She'll be fine as soon as we're gone. When she can't hear the car, she'll calm down."

I didn't believe him.

One day we were on our way to an ICU staff picnic. As soon as I'd closed the gate and we were driving, I asked Mark to stop the car a mile up the road. When he did, I got out and walked back to where I could see our yard. Misha was galloping around and shrieking. I sat behind a bush to watch her. An hour later she was still screaming, running, and looking down the road for our car. I called to Misha from behind the bush, skipped my hospital picnic and stayed home with her.

I could no longer enjoy going out with Mark. It was impossible to browse through antiques, or volley a tennis ball, knowing Misha felt sad and abandoned without me. If Mark and I ever hoped to go anywhere fun again, I'd have to find a way to bring Misha with us.

Back then, we didn't own a truck. When Mark needed to haul plywood or hay home, he borrowed our neighbor's truck. If Misha was going to travel with us, we would have to buy one. I knew she wouldn't like a horse trailer because she never wanted to be separated from us. And I didn't like trailers because they are cold, drafty, and dangerous. I was determined to find a vehicle the three of us could ride in together, something big enough so Misha would have room to move around.

For a long time, I nagged Mark about buying us a minivan. I wanted him to blow the top off of it and rebuild the roof high enough so Misha would have plenty of headroom (kind of like in the old "Flintstones" cartoon where Fred and Wilma take Dino to the drive-in and Dino watches the movie with his head stuck out of the roof, only Misha's head would be inside). Mark said what I was asking him to do was structurally impossible. If he blew a van roof off, the supporting metal would weaken and the van would collapse onto itself.

I bugged him about buying a pickup truck and building an enclosed wooden "room" on the back of it. But he said all the extra weight from the wood couldn't pass state vehicle inspections.

So Mark and I stopped going out together. It was easier on me to stay home than to leave Misha in misery. For a while, the only time I left was to go to the hospital. I did all my grocery shopping and household errands before clocking in for duty. Then one day on my way to work, I stopped at the Nickel's Thrift Bakery to get Misha a sack of treats and happened to spot a Nickel's Bakery truck parked in the back lot. The minute I saw it I thought, "Eureka! At last, I've found Misha's truck."

I walked over to it and looked inside. There was no wall separating the front of the truck from the back cargo area. Misha could stand behind the passenger seat, hang her head over my shoulder and watch the highway zip by out the front window. The back was roomy. She'd be able to turn around.

I raced inside the bakery and asked for the person in charge of trucks. The cashier pointed me to an enormous garage at the back of the store. In my meticulously clean, sterile-white nurse's uniform, I squeezed between tool chests, greasy hydraulic jacks, engine blocks, and girlie pinup calendars in search of the head mechanic.

He startled when I found him. I asked if he'd sell me a bakery truck. "Nah, we only sell them to other trucking firms."

"Do you ever make any exceptions? Wouldn't you even consider selling one to me?" I asked.

"You know how to drive these big trucks?"

"No. But the truck isn't for me."

"Well, who's it for?"

"My horse."

45

"Your horse? Is she gonna drive it? Or are you planning to put her in a pan, cook her and sell her as bakery?" he laughed.

"No, I want to haul her around in the truck, to take her places with me."

"So why don't you just buy a trailer?"

"Because I want her to ride with me, so we can be together."

Other mechanics started drifting over and formed a circle around me. They listened to my story. One of them asked if I was a nurse. When I said I was, he said to the head mechanic, "Go on, Dickie, you better sell this little lady her bakery van. You never know when you'll wind up in her hospital and it'll be her turn to take care of you. I find it's always a good policy to be nice to nurses and nuns."

Dickie said it was highly unorthodox to sell one of his commercial trucks to a person off the street , but since it was for my horse, he guessed he could probably push through the paperwork and make an exception for me. Dickie said I had to promise him I'd never try to represent myself as a Nickel's Bakery truck driver.

I gave him my word I wouldn't. He told me I could pick it up next week. As soon as I got into work, I called Mark and told him about the truck. He said it sounded perfect.

When we picked up the truck, I saw that Dickie had painted over the Nickel's Bakery logo. I asked him why. He said, "I'd never want anyone to be misled and think you worked for my bakery."

We thanked him and Mark started the engine. Dickie wished us good luck. "You drive over here with that horse of yours in my old truck and I'll give her some jelly doughnuts, free, on the house."

The truck rattled all the way home because the cargo bed was still filled with stacks of stainless steel bakery racks. There was only one seat, and the engine refused to go faster than fifty-five miles per hour. When we pulled down the driveway in our new, big, white, clanging box of a truck, Misha's eyes got huge. I jumped out and said, "Look. This is for you. Now you can go everywhere with us."

She walked around the truck several times, licked the windshield, jostled the license plate, then ripped the radio antenna right off the dash. "I guess she doesn't want to listen to music while she's riding," I said to Mark as he picked up and inspected the twisted, scrunched antenna metal.

Mark had a lot to do to make the truck safe for Misha. He welded in a passenger seat for me. He bolted a two-inch pipe to a ten-inch board and positioned them to act as a divider between the back of our seats and the cargo area of the truck. In case we ever had to stop quickly, the pipe divider would hold Misha back and keep her from slamming through the front windshield.

So Misha wouldn't flop from side to side, Mark bolted a twelve-foot-long pipe from the passenger seat to the back of the truck. He attached the back of the pipe with a hinge so when Misha is loading and unloading, the pipe can swing up out of the way over to the side of the truck. When we're ready to drive, the pipe swings back and is positioned parallel to her body. Another smaller pipe behind her tail keeps the side pipe tightly in place. This heavy-duty pipe cage encircles Misha's body, and in case of an accident, will hold her firmly in place and reduce her risk of injury.

The cargo bed of the truck is three feet off the ground. I didn't want Misha to have to leap up into the truck every time she loaded. So Mark built her a ramp made from sturdy locust posts and tough oak slats. The ramp leads from the ground into the truck's back entrance. When it's time to go somewhere, Misha walks forward up the ramp into the truck until she is positioned behind the passenger seat. I fasten the pipes around her while Mark pulls the ramp into the truck and stores it beside her.

The ramp is also used to unload her. Many people ask their horses to back out of trailers when it's time to unload. According to biologists, horses that live in the wild rarely walk backwards. It's an unnatural, abnormal movement for them and very hard on their muscles.

I thought Misha would be happier if she could turn, face the ramp, and walk forward to unload. The bakery truck is so wide she can turn 360 degrees without any difficulty.

Teaching her to load safely and enthusiastically took many days. The first time was easy. I laid corn inside the truck; she spotted it and walked right up the ramp to eat it. But the second time, she slipped on the metal floor of the truck; the third time, she lost her balance when she stepped off the ramp crooked. After that, she was frightened and refused to set one hoof near the truck.

I gave her a few days off and then tried again to load her. For the next three hours on an eighty-five-degree summer day, I coaxed, cajoled, and bribed her. She would not agree to even step onto the first ramp board. Mark threw up his hands in disgust and said, "What a stupid horse. I'm done with this. You deal with her," and walked away.

I'd read a lot of books on how to convince horses to do what you want them to do. I disagreed with almost all of the books' techniques. The basic horse-trainer school of thought went something like this: first you "whisper" to the horse; when that fails, you try to outsmart him; if that doesn't work, you resort to force (the old "Let them know who's boss" strategy). I decided to follow my own principles. Misha had to learn to trust me and do what I asked her to do, without question, because she had faith in my judgment.

I had to teach her to load all over again. I laid two thick carpets down on the cargo floor and a rubber mat on the ramp. That way she wouldn't slip or stumble. I filled my pockets with cookies. I attached my heavy-duty lead to her halter, walked her up to the ramp, heaped a pile of corn in the front of the truck, and held the lead taut so she couldn't back away. Then I started talking to her. As soon as she relaxed a little bit, I lifted one of her front hooves onto the ramp and rewarded her with half a cookie. After she let her hoof rest a while on the ramp, I got behind her and moved a back hoof. Sometimes she'd pull away and all her hooves would be back on the ground and I'd have to start all over again. Every time she rested a hoof on the ramp, she got a cookie.

Two hours passed before all four hooves were on the ramp. She advanced cautiously and was just about ready to walk a front hoof into the cargo bed when she took a good look inside at the dark, cavernous truck, got scared, and backed frantically out onto the ground. And so we went up and down, in and out, for a few more hours.

Mark came by a couple of times and told me I'd never coax her in. He said, "Misha is so much bigger than you; she knows she can overpower you. She'll never load just because you sweet-talk her."

I refused to listen. My success came because I eventually wore her out. She was so tired from lifting her hooves all afternoon and so hungry from not grazing that she gave up. She decided it would just be easier to do what I was asking her to do. All of a sudden, without any warning, she walked up the ramp, headed for the front of the truck, put her head down and munched her pile of corn.

I danced, squealed, whistled, and applauded. I gave Misha cookies and told her she was the most brilliant girl. As soon as she was done with her corn, I walked her up and down the ramp, in and out of the truck at least fifty more times until she lost her fear of loading.

Or so I thought.

Mark and I have always loved to swim. Since the first day we brought Misha home, we planned on teaching her to swim. We wanted to start her while she was still little. A week after we bought our bakery truck, the temperature soared to eighty-eight degrees. We decided that the day was our perfect opportunity to take Misha swimming. Salt Fork State Park, with its 3,000-acre lake, is only a thirty-five-minute drive from where we live, and seemed a perfect place for Misha's first outing.

We put our bathing suits on under our shorts and shirts, collected our sun block, towels, blankets, lawn chairs, and a three-gallon thermos of iced tea. We got everything loaded into the truck and locked up the house, barn, and garage. Mark positioned the ramp while I put a lead on Misha.

I walked her up to the ramp. She sniffed it, took a deep breath and strolled right into the truck. Mark said, "Wow, I'm impressed." He hopped inside to secure the pipes. All of a sudden, Misha turned, dashed down the ramp, and ran.

"What was that all about?" Mark asked.

"I haven't a clue."

Misha didn't get very far away because I was still holding onto her lead. I stood by her shoulder and pointed her back towards the truck. "Misha, I need you to load." She was scared and wouldn't budge. The whites of her eyes showed.

"What's the matter, good girl?" I asked. She tugged at the lead to pull away.

I tried repeatedly to load her. The thermometer was pushing ninety. Sweat had soaked through my clothes and underneath them, my bathing suit was wet and itchy. Mark got behind Misha several times and forcibly tried to push her up the ramp, but he couldn't move her.

After a while, Mark got fed up and said he didn't want to go swimming any more. He was going in the house to take off his bathing suit and turn on the air conditioner.

"Just give it up," he told me. "She'll never load into the truck today and you'll wind up dead from heat stroke."

I sat on the back edge of the truck while Mark unlocked the kitchen door and went inside. I heard the air conditioner go on. Misha was pulling tight on her lead, hoping to get away from the monster-ramp. As soon as Mark left, she calmed down and let the lead get slack. Next thing I knew, she was taking a standup nap.

I let her doze and regain her composure. Something had frightened her when she walked into the cargo bed. It was my job to reassure her the truck was safe.

The humidity had increased along with the temperature. I opened up our iced-tea thermos, poured half of it into a pail, and offered it to Misha. She gulped it down. I filled my sprinkling can with tepid water and poured it slowly over her neck and back. Then I wet a washcloth and wiped her eyes, nose, and forehead.

Tender loving care really can work miracles. By the time I finished fussing over Misha, she forgot to be scared of the truck. I said, "Are you ready to try again?"

She eyed the ramp and put her ears forward. "Go on, my girl, you can do it." She looked at me, gathered her nerve and marched into the truck. She was breathing hard as I fastened her safety pipes in around her. I raced into the house to tell Mark the good news. He was fast asleep on the couch.

I shook him awake. "Honey, honey, hurry, Misha's in the truck. She's waiting to go swimming."

"Forget it. I don't want to go now. It's too hot," he said groggily.

"Oh c'mon, don't be a party pooper. After all we've been through to get her loaded, we gotta go!"

Mark reluctantly put his swimming trunks back on. I went out and checked on Misha. Her nose was resting in the passenger seat and she was sleeping, but as soon as she heard me come around the door, she lifted her head and nickered. Then she stuck her tongue out and gave me a big, sloppy kiss.

Mark came out of the house and sat with Misha while I rushed around inside making some more iced tea. I heard Misha nickering back to Mark when he asked her why it took her so long to load.

When I came back out, Mark said, "Ladies, are we finally ready to go?" Misha and I nodded our heads in agreement. Then we pulled out of our driveway to take Misha on her very first swim.

Chapter Six

I t was ninety-three degrees when we finally got to Salt Fork. As soon as we pulled into the park entrance, I opened my passenger door so Misha could stick her head out and rubberneck the picnic tables and charcoal grills, the beach, the golf course, the tourists, and the youngsters playing softball. The fishy smells and the sounds of lapping waves added to her excitement.

Mark drove around the lake until he found a remote boat-launching site nestled in a cove. He parked the truck, set up the ramp and I unloaded Misha. Her brain was on high alert, her senses on overload from all the new odors to sniff and all the new sights to see. She couldn't decide what to do first: nibble at the strange species of weeds and bushes, paw at the shells in the sand, nudge the turtles tanning on the tarmac, or sample a taste of lake water. A great blue heron watched us set up our lawn chairs while hearty breezes tangled Misha's bangs, tail, and mane.

Mark and I stripped down to our bathing suits and sipped iced tea from tall plastic glasses. I let Misha off of her lead and she wandered around the boat-launching cove, tasting, smelling, listening, but with one eye always focused on me. I'd like to say our cove was beautiful and private, but it wasn't. Cars whizzed back and forth across a highway bridge running overhead and the shore was littered with twisted fishing line, hooks, diapers, beer cans, film canisters, and plastic six-pack rings. I was worried that Misha would cut herself on broken glass or swallow a metal pop pull-top. Mark told me to relax and let Misha enjoy her first day at the beach.

I went for a swim. The water was warm and when I floated on my back, fish nibbled on my toes. Misha walked to the edge of the shore and watched me. When I got too far out, she looked alarmed and whinnied. Mark yelled, "Stay there. I'll bring her out to you."

With a 20-foot lead hooked to her halter, Mark eased Misha into the lake. Her eyes got huge and her nostrils flared, but despite her fear, she followed Mark into the sloshing water. But as soon as the water touched her tummy, she refused to go any farther.

I called to her. Mark swam out away from her until the lead was taut. He tugged. She wouldn't budge. I swam towards her and helped Mark pull on the line. She took a few steps forward and stumbled off the raised sandy ridge into a deeper part of the lake. Now was the crucial moment—would she sink or swim?

Within seconds, she was dog-paddling, heading straight towards us. When she touched me with her nose, we applauded and covered her with wet kisses. She wanted to swim out farther, so Mark held tight to her line as she pulled him along behind her. She waded over to the other side of the shore, but instead of getting out, drank a couple big gulps of algae-flavored water and promptly fell asleep.

We gathered up our lawn chairs and set them in the water beside her. We sipped iced tea and read aloud while she slept. When Misha woke up an hour later, Mark was ready to go home. I wanted to take one more family swim before we left. Misha was worn out and didn't want to paddle back into the deep part, so we all bobbed around in waist-high water, Mark and I climbing over her back and under her belly.

When it was time to load, Misha wasn't sure she really wanted to go. She searched back and forth from the lake to her ramp, torn between more fun at the beach or the quiet calm of her comfortable porch. She flipped a few more shells around before walking herself up into her truck. Misha had decided on her own that there really was no place better than home.

The next time we took Misha swimming, several cars stopped on the bridge overhead. Parents and children got out of their vehicles, leaning way over the guardrail to photograph and videotape the dog-paddling Misha. The youngsters clapped and hooted, the adults gave us the high-five and thumbs-up sign. I was a little embarrassed to have so many people see me in my bathing suit, but Misha loved all the attention.

We took Misha swimming several more times that summer. One day a fisherman showed up with his two Labrador retrievers. For half an hour, the dogs and Misha swam together. Another time, a regatta of powerboats came speeding through our cove. As soon as the captains saw Misha, they turned off their engines, threw in their anchors and sat on their decks to watch her swim. She loved the water and loved to have people watching her. She was a natural-born, floating ham.

Swimming at Salt Fork was such a success we started taking her with us most everywhere we went. During the week, when the courts at the college weren't crowded, we liked to play tennis. The first few times Misha went to the college, I walked her onto the tennis courts with us. But it was obvious that the hot pavement and the scarcity of grass made her sweaty and bored. So eventually I let her run loose in the field beside the courts. She never wandered far. While Mark and I volleyed balls, she grazed with one eye on me.

Fall came. Faculty and students returned to the campus. When we played tennis around the noon hour, students would bolt out of the college cafeteria carrying apples, salad-plate-sized peanut butter cookies, and chunks of cherry pie, make a beeline for the tennis courts and come over to ask me if they could feed Misha.

At first I hesitated, thinking about the Halloween-time horrors of razor blades hidden in candy and rat poison injected into caramel apples. But it was hard to imagine these fresh-scrubbed students as dangerous or malicious. They wanted to feed Misha and Misha wanted to eat. I didn't have the heart to say no.

So while we played tennis, a steady stream of freshmen and sophomores left the lunchroom toting their desserts over to share with Misha. They never lingered long. They had classes to go to and books to read; their momentary joy came in watching Misha eat. As soon as she'd devoured their offerings, the students headed back to their classrooms and dorms. For Misha, playing tennis in the fall meant a smorgasbord of desserts.

The hardest times for Misha were still the evenings I had to go into work. As soon as she saw my uniform come out of the closet or heard me rip open a fresh package of white pantyhose, she worked herself up into a dither. Most days I did my grocery shopping before I went into work, which meant I had to leave an hour or two early. Misha would try to block the door so I couldn't get out of the house. When that failed, she stood behind the car so I couldn't drive away.

I thought it might be easier on her if she saw where I went when I got all dressed up in white. So on the weekends, whenever possible, we loaded Misha into her truck so she could help drop me off at work.

She hated to see me walk away from the truck. Mark said she nickered for me long after I was out of her sight. As soon as I got to the third floor, I stood in front of the big ICU windows to watch her. Misha's eyes were always focused on the hospital entrance doors. Even as Mark was driving away, she craned her neck backwards, still hoping to catch one last glimpse of me.

Mark and Misha often picked me up on Sundays, because I worked day shift and got off at 3 P.M. The two of them always arrived early. Right before I got off duty, I'd look out the ICU and see them parked in the patient drop-off circle watching for me. Misha's eyes were glued to the hospital doors. She would spot me coming through them even before the doors had closed behind me. She nickered and nodded her head. As far as she was concerned, I could never get over to her truck quickly enough.

A lot of times I'd get off duty and find a crowd of nursing technicians and LPNs surrounding the passenger door of our truck. Misha's head would be stuck way out watching for me while hospital staff tried to pet her. As soon as I wiggled my way through the sea of white uniforms, Misha stretched her neck out through the throng to give me a juicy, wet kiss.

One afternoon, just before quitting time, I looked out the ICU windows and saw a prominent neurosurgeon, his anesthesiologist, and a clinical psychiatrist encircling our truck, talking to Misha. I saw the surgeon pull a peanut butter energy bar out of his suit coat pocket, unwrap it and feed it to her. Even though she was busy chewing, her eyes were still glued to the hospital doors. The second I came out, she nickered and tossed her head. I jogged over to the truck and Misha kissed me. The psychiatrist said to me, "This must be your horse."

I said, "However did you guess?"

He chuckled. "Must be my incredible therapeutic intuition."

Some days we unloaded Misha and strolled around the hospital campus. Her favorite place was the hospice building because there were always lots of people and lots of food to be found. Every cancer patient's room opened up to the outside, and many Sundays found families sitting in lawn chairs under trees, visiting with their loved ones.

The hospice patients were always skinny and weak, so family members tried to fatten them up with special entrees and desserts they'd bring from home. But the patients had no appetite and usually couldn't eat more than a few bites. The chocolate eclairs, French sorbets and gourmet pizzas often sat on picnic tables fading and un-eaten. Then Misha would show up and beg.

The children especially loved her. Most were too young to understand death, and hospice was confusing for them. But that all changed when the big brown horse showed up. The kids howled with delight when Misha shoved her nose into a pizza box or chased jellybeans around the sidewalk. I had to be careful they didn't feed her all the food that was meant for the patients. I never let Misha have more than her fair share and finally I would stop the children by telling them, "Misha says, 'No thank you. I've had enough to eat.'"

The patients loved her robust hunger, her unbridled enthusiasm for all food, and the goodbye hugs she gave before she left. The atmosphere at hospice was often gloomy, but Misha brightened up everybody's day no matter where she went.

Another one of Misha's favorite places was the grocery store. She wasn't allowed inside, but that didn't dampen her passion. Mark and Misha stood outside the grocery store windows, watching me dash around to shop. They were still standing there when I reached the checkout. I always bought a few loose candy bars and tossed them into my grocery bags while I waited to pay.

The minute I stepped out of the store, Misha nosed through my groceries, looking for her Mounds, Baby Ruth, and Reese's Peanut Butter Cups. As soon as she got wind of the chocolate, she plucked the package out with her teeth and "handed" it to me to unwrap. She knew exactly how many seconds it should take to rip the wrap-per off a candy bar and if I took too long, she'd paw the pavement, unable to contain her excitement.

Sometimes while I was shopping, a bag boy or cashier would spot Misha peering into the store. Word would spread among the employees and before long, someone from produce would come out-side and offer Misha a few carrots or apples. The Little Debbie deliveryman stopped in the middle of restocking shelves to bring Misha half a case of Swiss Chocolate Rolls. One day a baker brought out a whole "damaged" banana cream pie. The crust had a split in it and the baker told Misha it was hers if she wanted it. "You look as if you might like pie."

A small crowd gathered to watch Misha push her soft, hungry lips deep into the foil pie plate. The onlookers "ooh-ed" and "aah-ed" as she devoured an entire pie in less than two minutes. As soon as the pie was gone, Misha gave the baker a sticky, cream-flavored kiss and resumed her post of watching for me through the store window.

Shoppers often stopped on their way out and asked Mark if they could feed Misha some Oreo cookies or some grapes. "Some? Are you kidding? Give her a chance and she'll stick her whole head in your grocery sack and take a comprehensive food inventory."

The day before Thanksgiving, Salvation Army volunteers were already standing beside red kettles ringing their bells. Misha tugged at me until I let her go over to see what was in the kettles. She peered down inside the first one and was shocked to find only money. Unless those coins were chocolate-covered, she wasn't interested. She dragged me to a second kettle and a third. Disappointment was written all over her face.

One of the bell ringers came over and asked me if Misha would like an apple. I said, "She'd love one." More Salvation Army workers wandered by with their apples and a few cupcakes. They said the Salvation Army always provided complimentary brown-bag lunches for the kettle volunteers and nobody much cared for the apples. They were glad to share the leftovers in their lunches with her. I slipped several dollar bills into a kettle before going back to the truck.

Ever since that day, whenever Misha hears Salvation Army volunteers chiming their bells, her saliva starts to flow and she looks around expecting leftover tidbit lunches.

Not long after that, I took Misha into our local mall. Using one of the side entrances, we walked by a restaurant, a shoe repair place, a video arcade, and a beauty salon before hitting the main shopping thruway. Busboys, cobblers, clerks, and beauticians left their stores to come out and stare at us. We were getting ready to pass by a jeweler's when two mall security workers materialized out of nowhere. "Stop," one of them shouted. "You know you aren't allowed in the mall with a horse. Get out right now."

The men frightened me and seemed unnecessarily harsh. I expected them to handcuff Misha to me and throw us both in prison. Misha was already nervous about her first visit to the mall. After the guards came over and yelled, her fear intensified. So when I headed her back down the side entrance and tried to walk her out the set of double doors, I couldn't get her through. We had no difficulty getting out the first door. But as soon as I managed to get the second door opened, the first door would smack her bottom since no one was holding it open. Because she was so nervous, the door closing on her rump scared her even more and instead of continuing forward, she'd back into the mall again. After several futile, frustrating attempts, the security men finally each held a door open for us so we could get out.

I thought maybe they were pretending to be mean and that as soon as Misha was out of the mall, they'd smile or offer a kind word. Horses weren't all that unusual in the mall because several times a year, shoppers could get their holiday photographs taken standing beside or sitting on a pony in front of one of the larger stores. So how irritated could the guards really be? Turned out they were a whole lot irritated. They walked us to our truck and told me if I ever brought Misha in again, I'd be in serious trouble. Who knew the mall was so pro-pony, anti-horse? That was the first and last time I ever took her inside a store or a shopping center.

Misha didn't care; she didn't even like the mall. Her favorite "shopping" spot was behind the grocery store. One day we decided to cut through traffic and drive around the back of several stores to avoid the construction up ahead. As we cruised behind a grocery, we saw a dumpster heaped to overflowing with corn on the cob. There were at least 100 ears, still in their husks, sitting at the same height as Misha's head. Mark pulled the truck up next to the dumpster. Misha stuck her head out the door, smelled corn, dove her nose into the dumpster and yanked out three cobs by their tassels. As soon as she finished eating those, she dove in again and pulled out four more.

I couldn't let her have too much fresh corn all at once for fear it might hurt her stomach. And no way would she agree to leave her corn treasure behind. So I lifted out most of the corn from the dumpster, heaved it into the back of the truck and let Misha eat it later that day and the next.

From then on, Misha always begged us to drive around to the back of grocery stores. One day she discovered a crate of slightly bruised peaches, and another time fifty-five tightly sealed bags of caramels. Dumpsters were my horse's dream come true—huge volumes of her favorite foods at a cost her "parents" could afford.

I wondered if food from dumpsters was sanitary. Until the day we found the corn, I didn't even know grocers threw away so much good food. When I asked some co-workers if they knew anything about dumpster food, they told me lots of poor, hungry people must "dumpster dive" every day just to have enough to eat.

"Why don't the stores give the food away to shelters and food pantries?" I asked. No one had an answer.

Mark and I didn't like dumpster diving, but Misha thought it was great. So, against our better judgment and ignoring our proclivity towards cleanliness, we let her pick fruits and vegetables out of dumpsters for several months, until the day we pulled up to a dumpster filled with day-old loaves of bread. I told Misha she could take home a couple packages, but she had to leave the rest for the hungry people. Misha had just completed her selection—six loaves of split-top butter raisin bread—when a grocery store employee burst out the back door, ran over to our truck and began shouting.

"I'm going to call the police on you."

"Whatever for?" we asked.

"It's illegal to be in these dumpsters. Can't you read the signs?"

"I've read all the signs. The signs warn me not to fall in because the dumpster is deep and I might have trouble getting out," I said.

"The signs also say you'll be prosecuted if we catch you stealing from this dumpster," she said.

There was no sign warning of prosecution. We didn't have a clue that dumpster diving was illegal.

I said, "We're awfully sorry. We didn't know it was against the law to take thrown-away food. Here's your day-old bread. My horse picked it out for her dinner."

The employee grabbed the loaves from my hand, slammed them inside the dumpster and banged the door shut as she went back inside the store.

Misha looked longingly at the bread. Fortunately, I always kept a package of Lorna Doone cookies stashed in the front of the truck to have as a reward. I dug out the cookies and offered them to her as a kind of consolation prize.

So ended our dumpster-diving days forever.

Chapter Seven

I nsects never much mattered in my life until I adopted Misha. Before she came, flies were a nuisance at picnics and mosquitoes were bothersome only at night. As long as the window screens fit tightly and the screen doors were latched, bugs stayed outside and were a non-event. Until Misha. She attracted zillions of flies and mosquitoes that I couldn't ignore because they had the potential power to kill my horse.

Misha wore a protective face mask during her first summer with me. I kept her slathered with bug repellent during the hottest months. I vaccinated her against encephalitis, tetanus, and certain strains of equine flu. But there was no vaccine to prevent equine infectious anemia (a fatal disease transmitted by the horsefly), Lyme disease, and other insect-borne viruses. By the end of September, I was able to breathe easier. Fly, tick, and mosquito season was over and Misha was still healthy.

I stopped applying her fly repellent. The nights were frosty and the days cool and breezy. Sometimes houseflies covered her neck and shoulders, but since they usually didn't transmit serious diseases, I wasn't worried. I still kept her fly mask on to protect her delicate eyes.

One mid-October afternoon I was mopping Misha's porch. All

of a sudden, she bolted through the door. She was restless, spinning around and acting odd. I said, "C'mon Misha, settle down, I'm trying to wash your porch."

Still, she kept pacing. I put down my mop and examined her for lacerations, wasp stings, a swollen ankle, anything that might explain her erratic behavior. I found nothing, gave up, and went back to mopping.

She couldn't relax. I fed her some graham crackers. She ate them distractedly. I poured her some Kool-Aid; she refused to drink. Something was definitely wrong. I got up on the couch so I could take a good look at her back. There at the base of her neck was a big, bulging, hideous horsefly. I screamed, grabbed it, and squished it with my foot. Half a teaspoon of Misha's blood squirted out of the fly's body.

I was angry with myself. How could I have ignored what Misha was trying to tell me? How could I let that fly suck her blood as she stood five feet away from me? Why did I ever send her out to graze without fly repellent? I apologized to Misha for my stupidity. She'd calmed down the minute I'd flung the fly off of her. I gave her a hug and went back to my mopping.

That evening, Misha's appetite was poor and her behavior was lackluster. She didn't nicker or kiss me. I wasn't overly concerned, though. I figured she'd worked herself up and worn herself down trying to outrun the horsefly and now she needed to rest.

The next morning, Misha's appetite was gone. Her eyes were dull. I knew she was sick. I smeared some petroleum jelly on the thermometer and checked her temperature. I couldn't believe my eyes. Surely it didn't really say 103.8 degrees? (Normal temperature is 100.5 degrees.) I rechecked it. This time it was 104. I hollered for Mark and asked him to ready the truck. I called the vet and said we were on our way.

By the time we got to the vet's, Misha was swaying on her feet. I walked her over to a patch of short grass and she nibbled unenthusiastically. The vet came out and said, "There's nothing wrong with this horse, she looks perfectly fine to me."

"Her temperature is 104," I said.

"No it's not. If it was that high, she'd be laying down and refusing to get up." I winced when he spit on his thermometer before inserting it.

"Jackie, is this your first horse?" he asked.

I nodded.

"I figured. You're just overly nervous. Horses hardly ever get sick. You worry too much. This horse is fine."

Three minutes later he removed the thermometer, wiped it off, shook it down, spit on it and reinserted it. "Why'd you put it back in?" I asked him.

"Had a false high reading. Gotta recheck it."

Three minutes later his thermometer still read 104 degrees. "Well," the vet said, "she must have a touch of the flu."

I told him about the horsefly bite the day before. "No," he said, "that's not why she's sick. She must have been exposed to another horse."

Misha hadn't been around other horses for months. But one thing I've learned from years of nursing is to never argue with a doctor (or a dentist or a vet). Even when I know they're wrong, I keep quiet.

"I'll give her a shot of penicillin and B vitamins and take some blood to test for EIA. But I gotta warn you, if she's not better by morning, she's probably not gonna make it," the vet said.

He gave her a shot in her shoulder, took a blood sample, charged me sixty-five dollars and sent us home. By the time I unloaded her and settled her onto her porch, Misha's shoulder was swollen and hot where the vet had injected his penicillin. Within an hour, the swelling had moved up towards her neck and clear fluid was weeping out of the hole left by the hypodermic needle. Her temperature was 104.4. She wouldn't eat or drink. When people get sick, modern medicine always has at least one more trick up its sleeve to offer. A patient can be two heartbeats away from death and some brilliant doctor somewhere will come up with a last-ditch miraculous treatment that will save the patient's life. But veterinary medicine hasn't kept pace with human medicine, and miraculous cures are rare.

Back then, I didn't know any equine-infectious-disease specialists. There were no emergency lifesaving techniques I could perform to make Misha well. All I could do was keep her comfortable and administer lots of TLC.

While Misha was sick I let her spend her nights on the porch. I scattered straw over her rubber floor and laid a heavy rug on top of it. I made the couch up into a bed so I could sleep on it. I woke up two times a night and walked Misha outside to do her business. There was nothing more I could do except watch and wait.

For three days, Misha wouldn't eat. If I filled a big syringe with Kool-Aid, she would swallow the liquid as I forced it down her throat. Otherwise she wouldn't drink. Her temperature never dropped below 103.7 degrees and she spent most of her time lying on the porch floor, looking like she was going to die. A few times, I managed to get some aspirin down her. One day she ate a few bites of tomato. But most of the time I laid on the couch staring at her, wondering if next I'd be burying her. In the middle of the night, I would coax her out to relieve herself under the cold starry sky. She was mildly dehydrated and wasn't making much urine. I had to encourage her kidneys to work.

The vet called to tell me Misha's blood test was negative for EIA. He asked me how she was doing. I told him her temperature was still 103.8. "That doesn't sound good," he said.

I neglected all my housework. Mark made his own meals and packed his own lunches. I told my head nurse I wouldn't be in to work. I couldn't read, watch a movie, or even listen to the radio. All my focus was on Misha.

At 5 A.M. on the fifth day of her fever, Misha lifted her head off the floor and nudged me with her nose. A few minutes later, she licked my arm. I leaned over and kissed her. She kissed me back. I offered her a green M&M candy and she ate it. I offered her a handful of M&M's and she ate them too. A couple of minutes later, she heaved herself up, shook the straw off her body and started eating her hay.

I darted up off the couch to take her temperature. I woke Mark up and said, "Look, Misha is eating!" I filled a bowl full of icy fruit drink and she drank it down. Finally, it was time to check the thermometer. It read 102.1.

All I could do was sit back down on the couch and cry. I understood for the first time what "tears of happiness" really meant. My girl was getting well. She wasn't going to die!

Children and animals make remarkably fast recoveries. One day they can lay prostrate, breathing shallowly in a state of febrile semi-delirium. The next day their fevers drop and within hours, they're hyperenergetic little imps. By day six, Misha was eating everything as fast as she could find it, chew it, and swallow it. She raced around the yard bucking and tossing her head. She nickered at every bird flitting past her and whinnied anytime she saw Mark. Her temperature dropped back to normal.

Her five-day illness changed our routine forever. She hadn't spent a minute alone the whole time she was sick. She got to sleep on the porch every night, and liked her sickroom arrangements. The first evening I tried to put her back to bed in her stall outside, she refused to go. She wanted to sleep inside with us all the time, not just when she was ill.

There had to be a way she could live permanently on the porch. I put my thinking cap on and devised a simple plan, but one that required a lot of hard work and training. Whether or not I could follow through with my plan was dependent on Mark's willingness to rebuild.

The next morning I let my husband sleep in late. I woke him up with his favorite breakfast: paper-thin crepes with warm cherry filling. After he'd eaten, I told him to lay back down and let his morning chores wait. I brushed his hair, slipped his feet into slippers and put his old Bob Dylan tape on to play.

"Okay, enough is enough," Mark said. "Fess up. What did you break?"

"What do you mean, what did I break?"

"You're being too sweet and nice to me. It can only mean you broke something into a million pieces, something that'll be a lot of trouble to fix," he said.

"Oh no, honey, I didn't break anything."

"What then? C'mon, spit it out, I know you're up to something."

"Well, actually, there is just a little project I was hoping you'd do for Misha and me."

"Oh no, here it comes. If it involves Misha, it's going to be a lot of work. Okay. Get it over with. Let me hear your latest plan."

Mark knows me so well he can almost read my mind. I stopped wasting his time and explained what Misha and I wanted. "I was hoping you would cut a doorway out in the north wall of Misha's porch and attach a door that swings both ways, in and out. Then I was hoping you would connect Misha's stall and paddock to the double-swinging door on the porch, kind of a long corridor of wooden fence that joins the two together. Once that's done, I'll teach her how to go out the door so she can get to her paddock and do her business. That way she can start spending her nights on the porch."

"Cut out the porch wall? I just built it!"

"I know, and I'm so grateful. But after living through those five days when Misha almost died, I don't want her to have to sleep outside all alone. What if she gets sick in the middle of the night? How can she tell me when I'm in here and she's out there? Besides, she never grows a winter coat. It's not healthy for her to be inside all day and out in the cold at night. And I nearly lost her. She almost died and..."

67

"Enough already," Mark said. "Let me sketch a few drawings, then you and Misha look at them and see if they meet with your collective approval."

How could I ever repay this man who makes all my dreams come true? Not a day goes by that I don't thank the heavens for Mark. There probably isn't any other husband who would help me have a house-horse.

When I first came up with my remodeled porch plan, I thought we'd buy a conventional door and attach it to the door jamb with industrial-sized double-swinging hinges. But when we got to the home improvement store (Misha waited outside in the truck), the doors we looked at were either too flimsy for Misha's head or too expensive for our budget. They didn't even sell the kind of hinges we needed. When we finally found the hinges at a specialty lumber store, the cheapest ones were over $150.

I was discouraged. "Why does everything have to cost so much? I guess there's no way we can afford this project. Poor Misha, she just won't be able to live on the porch."

Mark didn't say anything. He disappeared into his workshop as soon as we got home. An hour later he came out carrying more sketches and said, "I've come up with a design plan. I think I can make Misha's double-swinging door, hinges included, for less than forty dollars."

"You can? Really?"

"Yes. I'll just run into town for a few sheets of plywood and some three-quarter-inch threaded rod. It should only take me a couple of days before you girls have your new porch door."

Construction began the next morning. Mark sawed out a doorway through the existing log porch wall. He filled the opening with a sturdy homemade insulated plywood door that hinged open and closed via a seven-foot piece of threaded rod that ran lengthwise through it. He set several locust posts between the porch door and

Misha's stall, and connected it all with a board fence. When he was done, Misha's porch opened into an enclosed paddock that included her stall.

As soon as the construction phase was complete, I had to teach her to push open her double-swinging door to get outside when she needed to do her business. She had never had an "accident" in the house or on the porch, but I was always nearby to keep close tabs on her. Anytime I thought she'd been inside too long, I'd push her out and not let her back in until she had finished. If she was going to sleep on the porch, she would have to go outside of her own volition.

I was confident she knew where the bathroom was, but I wasn't sure she would go outside without my occasional promptings. Somehow, I had to teach her how to push Mark's plywood door open into her paddock and stay out there until she did her business. This was the single most challenging lesson I ever tackled during her thirteen years of training.

Her plywood door had springs that provided tension so that the door would close shut behind her. The tension caused me great concern, because if Misha pushed out her door but didn't get her body through the doorway all at once, the door would close on her. Misha might try to back up into the porch as the door swung against her. If she didn't back in quickly enough, the door might close on her neck. And if her neck got caught between the doorsill and the door, it might choke and strangle her. First she had to learn how to push the porch door open. Then I had to teach her to never back up onto the porch while the door was closing. Once she was headed out, I had to keep her moving forward.

Misha has always been a good student, happy when school is in session, eager to learn something new. She quickly understood that the strange new wooden porch door was her next lesson. I walked her in and out of the door a dozen times. After a short rest break, I smeared some peanut butter on the inside of the door. While she licked the peanut butter, I nudged the door open a few times so she would see that it moved. Then I guided her to the door and showed her how to use her nose to "bamm" it open.

I stood outside the door and called to her. Mark stayed inside to help Misha push her way out. While she watched, he bopped the door open with his fist. I waved a cookie around outside. Before long, Misha nudged the door on her own, opened it and stepped outside. Mark and I clapped and whistled.

We tried again. Misha didn't understand what it was she'd done that had pleased us so much. This time, her moves around the door were tentative. An hour later she still hadn't pushed through the door on her own. She started pawing out of frustration. I took Misha for a restful walk and told her we'd tackle the door later.

Back from our walk, we returned to the porch. On her second attempt, Misha pushed the door open and strolled out to her paddock. I called to her from inside the porch and she pushed right back in. Misha "got it"; the lightbulb went on in her head. She was so proud of herself that she spent the rest of the afternoon walking on and off the porch through her door.

Then it happened. Something must have interfered with her concentration, or maybe she got sloppy. For whatever reason, she didn't push herself all the way through the door, and it closed onto her neck. I gasped. Mark reached over and pulled the door away. My tone of voice changed to indicate danger. "Never, never, never let your neck get caught in the door, Misha. You must always push through and walk straight out," I said.

Having her neck lodged in the door flustered her, so we took the rest of the day off. The next morning we began again. I made her walk through that doorway 100 times before lunch and another 100 times before supper. By the end of the day, I was confident that she had learned everything there was to know about door safety. The rest was up to her.

Now it was time for her to move onto the porch at night. We

went to the carpet store and bought three eighty -square-foot extra thick and fluffy remnant rugs. We laid them on the porch, one on top of the other. That night I walked Misha out to her stall, where she ate her bedtime corn. I made sure she did her business before walking her back onto the porch. The house was dark. I set my alarm clock for 3 A.M., gave Misha a kiss, and went to bed. When my alarm rang, I got up, walked Misha outside to do her business, walked her back onto the porch, and reset my alarm for 6 A.M. Again I got up, walked Misha outside, and brought her back in.

I followed the same schedule the next night, but instead of leading Misha outside, I asked her to walk out by herself. At 3 A.M., I said, "Go on outside. It's time to go to the bathroom."

She didn't understand what I wanted at first. But then she seemed to think about it, pushed through her door, and went outside. At 6 A.M., when I again asked her to go outside, she did.

On the third night, I set my alarm as usual. This time, as soon as Misha heard me in the kitchen, she pushed through her door and walked outside. After that, I never had to wake up with her again. Twice a night she goes outside, munches some hay, does her business and comes back inside to sleep.

It's been over ten years since Misha last slept in her stall. She prefers to be splayed out on top of her porch rugs. Most nights she lies down for three ninety-minute sessions.

During the first week, I woke up every time she lay down. Now my subconscious is used to her noises, and I never hear her. She snores, whinnies, nickers, and runs in her sleep. Five years ago Mark put baseboards along the wall on Misha's porch; she ran so hard in her sleep that her hooves smashed the metal baseboards flat within a month.

I love to get up in the middle of a moonlit night, tiptoe over to her porch, and watch her sleep. Her head rests on the kitchen door threshold her tail is fanned out over her rugs. Sometimes I'll find her still standing, not quite ready to drop down. Then I plant a big kiss on her shoulder and breathe in her fresh, clean horseflesh. There's no better smell in this world than her skin. On nights when I can't sleep because I'm anxious or sad, I concentrate on listening to Misha's sleepy, snoring sounds. Her noises of contentment relax me, and lull me to sleep much more effectively than counting sheep ever could.

Chapter Eight

Weanlings generally don't cost much on the open market because they can't be ridden. Most people want to buy a horse they can ride right now; they don't want to wait three years for some little equine squirt to grow into its kneecaps and strengthen its weak back muscles. But I was glad I had two unfettered years to bond at eye level with Misha. I was in no hurry to leap onto her back. I maximized our "ground" time together and never let any learning opportunity go to waste.

I started her on a daily walking regime when she was just a few months old. My dad and paternal grandmother took regular ten-mile Sunday strolls and "short" five-milers during the week, so I guess walking long distances is in my genes. I hoped to share my love of walking with Misha and had visions of the two of us rambling over hills and dells, side by side, taking in the arboreal sights and smells. Mark wondered if horses would walk long distances beside a human. I could see no reason why they wouldn't.

Misha was still a foal when we began strolling around the neighborhood. She walked slowly and tried to taste every new bud and blade of grass. In the beginning, we rested as much as we walked.

But just before her first birthday, our pace quickened. It was time for more serious and strenuous workouts.

I bought high-mileage Saucony sneakers for me and four Easyboots for Misha. Easyboots are lightweight polyurethane "shoes" that slip over the horse's entire hoof. They come in five sizes and have adjustable straps that hold the boots in place. Unlike conventional steel horseshoes, Easyboots don't need nails pounded into the horse's hoof to stay on, and they provide a lot of cushion and traction.

Dressed in our new footwear, Misha and I started out at a slow two and a half miles per hour, then quickly pushed up to four and a half miles per hour. Lots of times I had to swish her along with a thin stick because she loved to drag her feet and linger behind me. I wanted her head to be even with my right shoulder at all times. After a few weeks of stick-swishing and gentle reminders, Misha gave in and kept up with me.

As she got older, it was hard for her to match my pace. If she tried to walk as fast as I did, she naturally sped up into a trot. Her trot was a little bit faster than my walk so if she trotted, I couldn't keep up with her.

That's when I started jogging. I'd never been a runner. I was one of those pudgy kids who hated gym class and avoided all sports. The first couple of times I ran beside Misha, my side hurt, my leg muscles burned, and I could hardly catch my breath. But within a month, she and I were jogging for half an hour every other day, and my body stopped threatening to keel over.

Misha loved having me trot with her. On days when she felt especially energetic, I'd hold onto her tail, run behind her, and let her pull me along at whatever speed she wanted. Hanging onto her tail made me a strong runner. I'd grab a handful of tail hair, take a deep breath, and hold on tight as she sailed us up one steep hill after another. I felt like a water skier attached to a powerboat.

I began losing weight without even trying. Soon I could trace the definition of my thigh muscles and race up a flight of steps without huffing and puffing. Misha was my aerobics buddy, my motivator, my own personal trainer. And as we jogged mile after country mile, our bond strengthened.

At first, my neighbors thought we were a couple of goofballs, a half-pint horse and an almost-plump, thirty-year-old registered nurse running around the lonesome dirt roads. Lots of farmers stopped to advise me that I was supposed to be on Misha's back, not beside her. One man said, "She should be getting the exercise, not you."

A horse breeder admonished me for spoiling her. "She's big enough now to ride. Just go easy. You gotta let her know you're boss. She'll think you're her equal if you run along next to her."

An older couple over the ridge leaned out their kitchen window and snapped photographs of us jogging on one especially perilous, snowy day. And once, a township trustee drove up to ask me if I was hurt.

"No, I'm fine. Why do you ask?"

"The way you're running instead of riding, I thought your horse might have thrown you," he said.

But after a few years of seeing a trotting horse and a jogging owner pass by their windows, my neighbors accepted our oddness and began waving heartily or tooting their car horns. We became a kind of local attraction.

I don't think Misha would have been able to stay so calm in the house without daily exercise. Around her second birthday, she had a growth spurt and was restless, fidgety and hyper for a while. Without our four-mile jaunts, she would never have been able to stand composed and quiet in the kitchen. Exercise pacified her and sharpened her mental focus. On rainy days when we didn't jog, I had to scold her more often than usual for bumping and jiggling the refrigerator, dribbling water on the floor, overturning pots and pans drying on the drain board, and chewing on the dishtowels.

I started walking her around with a saddle on her back about the time she turned two. I used to be horse-ignorant and didn't know that a horse could be ridden bareback all her life. I thought saddles were necessary to trotting, galloping, and jumping. But after a few months, I discovered on my own that saddles were more of a nuisance than an aid.

Thirteen years ago, I relied too heavily on riding books. I followed their instructions for lunging by standing in the middle of a circle and making Misha trot around me while the stirrups banged against her sides. Circle work is hard on young horses and can cause irreparable injuries to their growing joints. I also made her walk over plastic bags, tires, and tree trunks so she'd get used to the "real world." But I would not listen to the experts when it came to bits. No matter how many books told me bits were necessary for control, I refused to put one into Misha's mouth.

Young horses make sense of their world the same way toddlers do; everything new goes in their mouths unless it's too big to fit. If it doesn't fit, they give it a good lick with their tongues. A horse's mouth means everything to it.

When Misha was a yearling, she stuck her nose into my vest and pulled out my handkerchief. I wasn't paying attention, and when I stooped down to pick it up, the handkerchief wasn't on the ground. I looked over at Misha. Her cheek was bulging. I pried open her mouth and saw my handkerchief poised and ready to head down her throat. Mark came and stuck his arm deep into her mouth and yanked the handkerchief out. In those few seconds, she had shredded it into tatters.

Misha's mouth is more sensitive than mine is, and I can only imagine how awful *I* would feel having a piece of cold metal jammed between my cheeks. If Misha eats something too hot, a big gray blister forms on her tongue or lips. If she bites down on something hard, she winces with pain. She can separate a metal twistie from a pile of corn, or pick a single aspirin out of a peanut butter, banana, and jelly sandwich. And she chews gum for hours.

When Mark is farming, he quenches his thirst by stuffing his mouth full of Wrigley's gum. He's such an anti-litterbug that he never throws his gum down on the ground when he's done with it. Before we got Misha, he always brought his gum home and threw it in the wastebasket. It was when Mark and Misha were building fence together that Mark first noticed that Misha was enormously attracted to the gum in his mouth. She'd lay her nose against his lips to inhale his chewing gum. Finally, Mark came in from the hayfield one day and dropped his six-stick wad of gum on the kitchen counter in front of Misha instead of throwing it away.

Misha didn't hesitate to pick it up and start chewing it. I worried she might choke, but she was having so much fun, I let her be. I went back to my housework. Ten minutes later, I came around the corner and saw she was still chewing that same wad of gum. Every time it dropped out of her mouth, she'd search the rug in front of her until she found it. Then she'd start chewing the gum all over again. Even today, she will work a wad of gum for two hours or more. I always end up taking it away from her before she tires of chewing it.

Once I saw how important Misha's mouth was to her, bits and hackamores were out of the question. Misha would have to wear only her halter when I rode her. Of course, as she grew bigger, she would grow spunkier. Trying to maintain my control over her would become a monumental challenge. It would have been a lot simpler on me to yank her around by a bar of steel in her mouth; instead, I had to rely on firm persuasion.

I started riding Misha a few months before her third birthday. She didn't mind having me perched on her back, but the saddle aggravated her horribly. As soon as I flopped it over her, she'd lower her hind end so the saddle would slip off. She'd reach around and yank the saddle with her teeth. And when I tried to tighten the cinch strap, she'd push her stomach out to enormous proportions so that later, when she breathed normally, the saddle would be loose and fall off.

I loathed lugging the heavy saddle around, with its cold, metal, clanking stirrups and tangled cinch straps, and the saddle pad weighed down my arm and made me itch. It was tough slinging all that gear over her back and trying to get it positioned tightly. I was worn out before I had ridden two steps. And I hated the creak and wiggle when I tried to mount. But the part about the saddle I hated the most was not being able to feel Misha's powerful muscles under me.

Riding her bareback, I can always tell ahead of time when Misha plans to move forward, balk, lurch sideways, or freeze with fear. Her back muscles "talk." Through my buttocks, I can feel how she is physically reacting to what she is seeing and thinking.

I tried riding her in a saddle for a few weeks. Then one day a piece of leather strap broke off. The saddle twisted, slipped down around Misha's side, and I tumbled, in slow motion, to the ground. That's when I decided saddles were useless, dangerous, and dulled all my tactile communication with Misha. I'd become a better, safer rider without all that leather.

I sold my three used, hand-me-down saddles and used the extra money for fly repellent and Nickel's day-old treats. Nine years later, my quadriceps and gluteus maximus are firm and defined. While my upper body has grown flabby with age, my lower body is strong and taut. My derriere is smaller than it was a decade ago. My waist, on the other hand, has expanded by two inches. Without a saddle to depend on, I've developed muscle masses that keep me on Misha's back whether she's leaping straight up in the air from fright or sliding down a muddy hill, using her front hooves as a sled. No matter how fast or irregularly we ride, I never fall off. In a split second, I can "read" her subtlest mental changes. After so many years, it's become second nature for my rump to interpret Misha's muscle movements and my brain to react accordingly.

In the beginning, I never rode her too far or too long. I didn't want to strain her muscles or overexert her knees. Until she was four, I never sat on her back for longer than twenty minutes three times a week. But because I rode her so gently, I could never completely tire her out. We still jogged together. I was exhausted after four miles, whereas Misha was barely warmed up. She could outrun me, outpace me, outdo me every time. I had to find an alternative way to expend her young-horse pep. Around her third birthday, I invented "speedwork."

When we first married, Mark bought us a small, inexpensive motorcycle, thinking it would be perfect for short jaunts to the tennis courts, video store, and libraries. We drove around on the bike for a few years without incident. Then one day a nurse who worked in my ICU was killed while riding on the back of her boyfriend's motorcycle.

After my co-worker was killed on her bike, I refused to ride on Mark's motorcycle any more. Our dirt roads weren't dangerous, but the paved roads scared me. If our heads hit the pavement, we would be killed. Mark agreed to put the bike up on blocks and let our license plates expire. The motorcycle sat idle for several years until I dreamed up speedwork.

I hooked a twenty-foot-long heavy-duty cloth lead to the left side of Misha's halter, then sat in the seat behind Mark on the motorcycle. I kept Misha's head lined up with my shoulder and held her lead in my right hand. As Mark slowly accelerated the motorcycle, Misha walked beside us. After half a mile, Mark sped up until she was trotting.

I kept Misha close to the bike at all times. I had the extra fifteen feet of lead coiled loosely in my lap. In case Misha stumbled or balked, I had a lot more lead I could unfurl in an instant. I always had my eyes glued to Misha during speedwork, watching her for signs of fatigue, muscle strain, confusion, or panic. Mark's policy was to stop the motorcycle any time a car came our way. We developed hand signals so I could immediately alert him to any changes in Misha's needs. He was too busy keeping the bike steady and safe to try to figure out what I was attempting to say over the roar of the two-cycle engine.

Squeezing his waist was my signal to stop. Patting his waist meant go faster. When I bounced up and down on the seat, it meant Misha was balky and we had to be on high alert. Two or three times, especially as a four-year-old, Misha wanted to see which was stronger—the bike or her. Twice she pulled the motorcycle down onto its side while Mark and I were sitting on it. We got some scrapes on our legs, but Misha wasn't hurt. We never worried too much over our safety; our focus during speedwork was always on her.

Some days she wore her Easyboots. But when she sped up to a canter, the boots would often fly off. So whenever the roads were muddy or wet, she did her speedwork bare -hooved.

Most of the time Misha trotted casually and willingly beside the bike, up and down the dirt roads, in all kinds of weather, with me cheering her on. "C'mon, good girl, you can do it. Just a little bit faster!" She enjoyed the hard exercise because she had so much childish energy. She was especially fond of speedwork because we did it as a family.

At four years old, she'd break into a canter to climb the steep half-mile hill to our house. On flat roads, she averaged seventeen miles per hour. When she felt especially frisky, she'd gallop at twenty-four miles per hour for a quarter mile. I never pushed her to go that fast. We let her set the pace and Mark accelerated the motorcycle accordingly.

Speedwork would not have been necessary if Misha hadn't lived in the house. But because she wanted to spend her days in my kitchen, she needed hard exercise.

Back from speedwork, I showered her off with piping hot water before letting her into the field. Sometimes she'd roll in the mud and I'd have to wash her off again. She'd do her business, nip at a few branches, then saunter into the kitchen, where I always had an enormous bowl of steamy cooked oatmeal sprinkled with brown sugar and cinnamon waiting for her as a reward.

Speedwork enabled Misha to succeed as a house-horse during her teenage years (ages three to four). Without that rigorous exercise, she couldn't have stood peacefully in the kitchen. Her natural youngster ebullience would have fussed, pawed, fiddled, and gotten her into trouble. I would have spent my days yelling, "No, No, No," all the time. Too much scolding would have been bad for Misha. It would have destroyed her self-esteem. Speedwork boosted Misha's physical and psychological confidence and gave her an angelic calm so she could live comfortably inside the house.

Chapter Nine

Everyone I knew thought that I'd eventually tire of having Misha inside the house. My friends and relatives figured I was going through "a horsey phase" and as soon as Misha was full-grown, I'd make her move outside. "After all," my father-in-law asked, "who ever heard of a horse in the house?"

His reaction was typical. All my life, whenever I've talked about animals, people have given me The Look, that nonverbal stare that tells me without telling me that they think I'm kind of weird. Folks have always been suspicious of me and my "funny way with animals." In elementary school, my favorite subject was biology. My mother encouraged my interest by enrolling me in advanced summer school science classes. Last year I was flipping through my old report cards and found some of my summer school evaluations. Report after report, each teacher made the same comment, "Although she's an excellent student with a strong scientific mind, Jacqueline has unrealistic expectations of animals. She assigns inappropriate emotions and feelings to them which suggest she's psychologically immature for her age group." My empathy with animals extended to my diet, and at age thirteen I gave up eating meat. I've been a committed vegetarian ever since.

My belief that animals feel pain, love, and loneliness certainly did not originate with Misha. It's not as if I woke up one morning and decided it would be lovely to have a horse in the house. It happened because Misha communicated her needs for warmth, protection, nurturing, and love to me. Luckily I was listening to her message, as I'd listened to the messages of other animals before her.

So when, out of the blue, without any warning, Misha started defecating on the porch, everyone I knew was eager to gloat and remind me that "animals are just animals." Lots of people took great pleasure in telling me it was about time I moved Misha outside. My next-door neighbor said, "You tried to make your horse into a human. You should have never brought her in your house to begin with. Everyone knows you can't toilet-train a horse."

For four and a half years, Misha had been perfectly housebroken. Even as a yearling, she'd never had an accident. If she turned towards the outside door and for some reason couldn't get out, she pawed ferociously until Mark or I came and opened up the door for her. She was fastidious almost to the point of obsession, and she'd rather let the urine float up to her eyeballs than urinate in the house.

Then one cold March morning, I woke up and found a pile on her porch rugs. I shouted at Misha and stormed around the porch. I flung the pile out the door and pushed her into the paddock with it. I told her she was bad and if she EVER did that again, she'd be living outside.

It's hard to yell at someone who loves you so much. She knew she had displeased me and was visibly upset. She huddled in her stall, ears and eyes spooked, every little noise making her jump. I couldn't stay angry for long. Within half an hour, I invited her back into the kitchen.

I couldn't imagine why she'd had an accident. Maybe she'd overslept, been bothered by a bad dream or had trouble getting out of the porch door in time. Whatever caused it, I knew she hadn't done it deliberately. I tried to put the incident behind us and we resumed our normal daily life.

The next morning I woke up to another pile on the porch. As soon as Misha saw me looking at it, she bolted out the door before I could start yelling. She knew she'd done wrong. I grabbed the broom, chased her around the paddock and berated her for the mess she'd made.

Four mornings in a row I woke up to accidents on the porch. My anger fizzled itself out. Instead, I was disappointed, devastated, and inconsolably sad. For some reason, Misha had forgotten her house-breaking. Family and neighbors made it worse by chiming in to say, "I told you so." Except for Mark. He gave me a million bear hugs and said I'd done the best I could.

What were my options? I couldn't just throw Misha outside to live. The nights were harsh and she wasn't used to freezing temperatures after sleeping on her porch for four years. I had no choice except to tackle this latest problem and find a solution. There had to be a reason why she couldn't hold her bowels long enough to make it outside. There was no way I was going to give up on Misha.

The next night, I slept out on the porch with her. I kept a 25-watt bulb burning and stayed awake most of the time. At 2 A.M.., Misha dropped onto her rugs to sleep. At 3:30 she stood up and in the next split second, had an accident. She looked over at me in a panic, as if to say, "Oh no. I didn't mean to, it just slipped out."

I didn't scold her. I saw that her accident was just that: unintentional and not her fault. She wasn't being "bad" or careless. Something out of the ordinary was happening in her intestines, and since I was the nurse and she was the horse, it was up to me to find the cause and the remedy. I cleaned up the mess, calmed Misha down, and went back to sleep on the couch. I woke up at 6 A.M.. Misha was sprawled out on her rugs snoring. I wiggled her back and forth to wake her. She sat up in a semi-recumbent position before heaving herself onto her legs. Just in time, I pushed her through the porch door.

"Whew, Misha, that was a close call," I said.

I was exhausted for the rest of the day, since I'd been up and down all night on the porch with Misha. I kept racking my brain to find a reason for the change in her habits, but I was too tired for any effective brainstorming. I decided if I was ever going to solve the problem, first I needed a good night's sleep.

So rather than spend another night on the porch, I laid a protective rubber sheet on top of Misha's rug, right on the spot where her rump rested when she's lying down. Misha prefers to sleep in pitch dark, so I turned off the nightlight. When I woke up the next morning, I could see Misha was agitated before I even got to her. There, on top of the protective sheet, was another pile.

I cleaned up the porch, comforted Misha, and got on with my day. While I scrubbed, cooked, ironed, and washed windows, I went through lengthy mental lists of possible bowel diseases, stomach disturbances, behavioral problems, and dietary changes.

Then, all of a sudden, the lightbulb went on in my head. Dietary changes! A month before, we had taken an inventory of our second-cutting hay and saw we were running low. We called up our hay suppliers. Because the winter had been hard and long, they were out of second-cutting. They only had fifty bales of first-cutting hay left if we wanted to buy those instead. We lugged them home. I started feeding Misha first-cutting during the day and second-cutting at night, thinking that by rotating the hay, the second-cutting would last longer until the grass turned green.

Introducing first-cutting hay into her digestive tract had to be the cause of Misha's recent incontinence. Now it all made sense. The grass that's cut first grows coarser, taller and stringier. The grass that sprouts up after the first cutting is taken off is more tender, succulent, and shorter. It was as if I'd started feeding bran cereal to a horse that was used to Trix. First-cutting hay bulked up her colon and increased her need and urge to defecate.

How could I have been so stupid and not figured this out before? Was there anyone in this world more ignorant than I? Here I was, yelling at my girl for something that was my own fault.

I immediately stopped feeding her the first-cutting hay. Within two days, her bowels were back to normal and she was again completely housebroken. In fact, after that episode, she was more careful and walked even farther out into her paddock away from her porch to do her business. She seemed as happy as I was when I removed her protective sheet. I bleached and scrubbed the offending spots on her rug so she wouldn't have any leftover fecal odors to bother her at night.

This incident strengthened our bond and improved our horse-person communication. Misha learned she could trust me, even when I was hopping mad. I learned that if I listened to her, she'd help me to understand what she was trying to say. Like people who speak different languages and use hand signs to communicate, I learned to take the time to decipher her message.

When Misha was seven, she had another short bout of incontinence on the porch. This time I didn't freak out. I laid down a protective sheet, then made a mental inventory of all the food she'd recently eaten. Three days before, I'd been picking up stray ears of field corn in a farmer's field to feed to the deer and squirrels in the winter. While I stuffed my bags, Misha nibbled beside me. I hadn't paid too much attention to her because I assumed she was finding and eating leftover corn. When I finally thought to look over at her, I saw that she was eating wet, dead corn stalks and leaves.

I walked her out of the cornfield, worried the stalks might be moldy or rotten, and stuck her on a patch of grass. Then I forgot about the incident until she had her "accident." Figuring three days was probably about how long it would have taken those corn stalks to reach her lower intestine, I was betting that as soon as she passed them, her bowels would clear right up.

Sure enough, four days later her intestines were back to normal. I removed her protective sheet. Even though I scrubbed up the spot on her rug, she avoided lying anywhere near it. For over a month, she slept with her neck and shoulders scooted out over the kitchen threshold, using the kitchen linoleum to pillow her head.

I've learned to be cautious about letting Misha eat too many fibrous plants. I don't give her a lot of brome grass or first-cutting hay, oat or wheat straw, peanut shells, or cornhusks. If I decide to eat a bowl of Raisin Bran cereal, I do it when Misha's outside. By limiting her bulk and crude fiber, I can rest assured that she'll never have another accident on her porch.

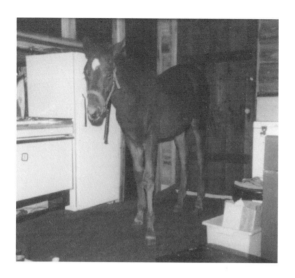

Baby Misha.

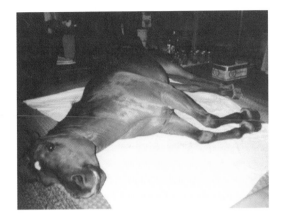

Misha taking a nap

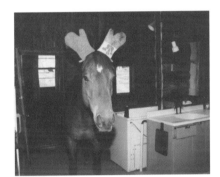

Helping out in the kitchen.

Enjoying one of her favorite meals.

Bath time.

Misha, Jackie and Rodent.

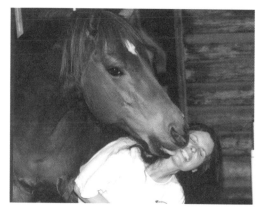

Getting a kiss.

90

Mouse

Dee Dee Myers

The Tresl family.

Chapter Ten

As soon as we'd bought the Nickel's Bakery truck, we'd started weighing Misha. I wanted an accurate weight so I'd know exactly how much worming medicine and antibiotics to give her and to keep track of how much she was growing. It was lots of fun pulling up into the century-old feed and grain store, unloading Misha onto the rickety scales and waiting while some crusty, dusty corn handler calibrated her poundage.

The first few times I'd asked the store to weigh her, the employees and loitering farmers stared at me like I was daft. But after a while, their moods changed and everyone at the grain store looked forward to our bimonthly visits. It became a community event. We'd

drive up, pull out Misha's ramp, and even before I got her unloaded, someone would shout, "Need her weighed today, do you?"

Inside the weight room, a grain employee would balance and adjust his scales and before long, he'd stick his head through the open window and call Misha's weight out to me and to the crowd that had gathered around us.

The scale fascinated Misha. There were always leftover bits of corn and oats laying on it and dozens of sparrows, pigeons, and crows milling around, hoping to steal some of the grain. Meanwhile, the grain store's resident cat hunkered behind the scale, hoping to leap out and snatch up an unsuspecting, hungry bird.

Misha was full-grown by the time she was four. After that, she never got any taller than sixteen hands and her hooves would always measure five inches across. Her height and length were set for life. Unfortunately, she continued to get wider. Her belly refused to stop growing. In less than nine months, she gained 105 more pounds and her waist went from eighty-one inches to eighty-six inches. On her fifth birthday, she weighed in at 1,430 pounds.

Because she had been starved as a weanling and had suffered such poor health, it never dawned on me that Misha was a prime candidate for obesity. Until she turned five, I'd never seen any reason to cut back on her desserts or limit her alfalfa hay. I had been diligent about exercising her, but I'd done it so she'd be calm, not slim.

Then, one day at the library, I found a new horse book. It contained a chapter on fat horses. Since I would never have to worry about Misha becoming fat, I decided to skip the text of the chapter and skim over the pictures. Flipping through the pages, my eyes focused on a photo of a horse with a ridge running down its back. The caption underneath said, "A ridge along the back means the horse is overweight. The deeper the ridge, the fatter the horse."

Misha'd had a ridge running down her back for a year. Who knew it meant she was too fat? And I wouldn't even care that she was fat except that I wanted her to live a long and healthy life. Obesity would increase her risk of heart, kidney, and joint disease. If I let her get too heavy, her life would be shortened.

I cut back on her Nickel's Thrift Bakery desserts. I used apples and carrots as treats and rewards. Instead of giving her a plateful of spaghetti, I gave her a small dollop. I substituted pretzels and hot-air popcorn in place of potato chips, and I stopped dribbling Mark's gravy over her pasta and rice.

Before putting her on a weight reduction program, I used to walk her along the roadsides to the damp places where lush clover and bird's-foot trefoil grew. I'd read my book for an hour while Misha grazed up and down the road. When she started her diet, I stopped the roadside nibbling. I also limited the time she could graze in the yard and when fall came, I changed her hay from an alfalfa mix to plain orchard grasses.

But reducing her calorie intake wasn't enough. Her body compensated by slowing down its metabolism. The fewer cookies she got, the less energetic she was. The less energy she had, the fewer calories she burned. So even though I was feeding her less, she didn't lose any weight.

Every few days I would wrap a dressmaker's tape measure around her belly. After two months of eating less, her waist went from eighty-six inches to eighty-five and a half. At that rate, she wouldn't get to eat another doughnut until she was 47 years old! I had three choices. I could let her get fat, I could never let her eat goodies again, or I could increase her exercise. I chose exercise.

Mark had long since tired of speedwork, so Misha hadn't run beside the motorcycle in over a year. I still jogged with her, but making her run at my pace of six miles per hour didn't do much to help her burn off many significant calories. I was already riding her about ten miles a week. I enjoyed being on her back but I didn't want to go overboard. It didn't seem fair or practical to over-ride her in my attempt to skinny her down, since doing anything in excess can be dangerous. So I decided to mix and match equine exercise regimes, tailoring them to fit the specific needs of my horse and me.

I was also hopeful that *I* could lose a little bit of weight. I had delusions of dropping down to 105 pounds and being Twiggy-thin for the first time in my life. I thought Mark would love me even more if I could fit into a size 7 pair of jeans. So Misha and I dieted together and started our own long-distance walking, jogging, and horseback riding triathlon. We always won the contest because no one but us competed.

Three times a week, Misha and I set off on foot, walking fast and running slowly for six to eight miles. Then, when my knees started to hurt and my energy was spent, I jumped onto Misha's back and she cantered me home. After a while, I began walking farther and farther. I kept a paperback book of poems in my pocket and when we'd gone as far as my knees would take me, we'd stop and rest in a field. Misha would graze while I read poetry. For a year, I pushed myself to travel longer and longer distances. Eventually I forced myself to jog most of the way back home instead of cheating and stealing a ride from Misha.

Our most grueling walks came every other Sunday when we traveled the nineteen-mile round trip to the college, leaving at 10 in the morning and dragging back home around 6 or 7 P,M.

Misha was an energetic five- and six-year-old and always eager to venture out with me. I'd make Mark's lunch for him to eat later, put Easyboots on Misha, stick my poetry book and a few dollars in my pocket, and off we'd go. Most of the way to the college was on dirt roads. But in the middle of our trip was a two-mile stretch of a busy state route.

At first, the cars and trucks racing by Misha on the paved road scared her. A one-mile-long guardrail kept us trapped along the berm and we couldn't get off the road when big, loud vehicles passed. The coal trucks were the worst. They used the same short section of road we did when they hauled their coal to town. The coal shook and rattled as it whizzed by us. A few times Misha ripped herself out of my grasp and ran to the other side of the road. As soon as the coal-truck drivers saw how nervous they made her, the coal trucker who was first in line would radio the truckers behind him and warn them that Misha and I were up ahead. Then every truck after the first one would slow down and ease gently past us.

After a while the trucks stopped bothering her. She'd just flatten her ears and keep right on jogging. Once we were back on the dirt road, we could slow down a bit and enjoy the scenery. We often rested at the Pitts' farm, where four regal Percheron workhorses were living out their retirements on a 50-acre pasture. The Percherons got so used to our every-other-Sunday walks that they started watching for us. As soon as they saw or smelled Misha coming, they'd whinny and gallop to us. Misha would whinny back and we'd stop so they could visit.

I used to think Misha was big, until she stood next to the workhorses. Percherons' chests are built like hulls of a ship, and their feet are as wide as soup bowls. I couldn't ever imagine having a workhorse living in my house.

A few times, the Percherons' owner, Mr. Pitts, walked down through his field to meet us. He was eighty-three years old and had farmed with horses nearly all his life. In 1984, he broke his arm and could no longer heave the harnesses up onto his horses. He was forced to buy his first-ever tractor. By the time I met him, he hadn't farmed with his Percherons in ten years. He invited me down to the barn to see his horse-drawn cutter, rake, and plow. All the tracings, harnesses and tack were clean and shiny, organized and hanging from railroad pegs punched into the old barn walls.

Mr. Pitts said what worried him most is what would happen to his horses when he died. He figured they'd outlive him by a decade or more. "My Mrs. don't like 'em because she's scared of 'em. My kids live in the city and they don't want 'em. I'd hate to see 'em get sent off to the meatpackers."

I offered to stop by every once in a while to make sure he was doing okay. If he needed any help with the horses, I told him I'd send Mark over. "And when your time comes, I'll do what I can to find your Percherons a good home."

Tears welled up in Mr. Pitts' eyes. "You don't know how much that means to me. Thank you." He reached over and buried his face in Misha's mane.

A little farther down the road was a yard full of goats and ponies that lived very sad lives. It was hard on me to stop so Misha could visit them. The ponies nickered for her when we jogged by and if we didn't stop, they'd let out a chorus of pathetic-sounding whinnies. Misha was the only bright spot in their otherwise dismal existence. The ponies had no trees, outbuildings, or lean-tos to protect them from scalding sunshine, biting flies or blizzard winds. Rusted-out cars and trucks littered their small, overgrazed field. I never saw them get a bale of hay, a bucket of grain, or a salt block. Sometimes the ponies got so excited to see Misha that they got their hooves caught in the rusty, barbed wire fencing. When they'd try to yank free, the fence would drag behind them, wrapping tightly around their ankles and legs and cutting their beautiful horseflesh to tatters. Eventually I had to avoid the ponies and the goats. Their living conditions were too cruel a sight for us to witness. It was almost impossible to block out their mournful wails as we jogged by.

Two miles before the college was a rental house filled with students and dogs. The students liked to have lawn parties and sometimes in the summer they would be outside eating and playing music when we passed by. Misha could smell the grilling hot dogs, the potato chips, pizza, and pop long before we got to the house so that by the time we were even with their yard, her saliva was dripping and she was ready to eat.

As soon as the first student spotted her, the whole bunch of students would come over and ply her with food and pop. They let her drink grape soda right out of their bottles. She thought that was extra special because I always made her drink her beverages out of a bowl. The pop would spill all over her face so that later, after we'd left the students, if she stuck her tongue out really far, she could lick her face and still taste her sweet, sticky, purple pop.

They always invited us to come join their parties but, being a square, middle-aged housewife, I declined their kind offers. Besides, we were supposed to be exercising, not lounging around at a gala get-together. I thanked them for the food and drinks they shared with Misha and, ignoring her protests, we continued on to the college.

It took us about three hours to get to the campus from home. My feet were always sore and I was happy to sit down. In the middle of the college, tucked behind the football stadium and the seniors' dorms, was a barbecue pit and covered picnic area situated in an isolated quarter acre of woods. That was where Misha and I always rested. I'd take my shoes off and sprawl out on the sun-dappled picnic table while Misha drank from the narrow stream and grazed. Sometimes I fell asleep. Misha stayed close by.

A few times we were interrupted by upperclassmen practicing their golf swings on the nearby woodsy path. Once we nearly fell over a young couple kissing. But usually we were alone. Rabbits and robins were our most frequent visitors.

On the last day of the spring semester, I heard five young women trooping down to the picnic area. I shook myself awake and checked to make sure Misha was out of their way. But instead of walking past her, they formed a circle around her. One girl said, "We're from that dorm over there." She pointed up over the hill. "My friends and I have seen you and your horse here so many times and we were just wondering what you do here? I mean, it is kind of boring, isn't it, just a picnic table and some grass?"

I told her that Misha and I used the center of their campus as our rest stop. I said we lived almost ten miles away and that we took long, adventurous walks together. "My horse and I are making memories."

The girls giggled. A tall blonde said, "We came out here to invite you and Misha into our dorm. Everybody's mostly moved out and we thought it would be awesome to have a horse in our dorm the day before we graduate."

"Misha would love to come into your dorm," I said.

So the seven of us walked up the hill and through the front door of the seniors' residence. The girls asked me if I would let Misha loose. I said, "If it's okay with you, it's okay with me."

For the next hour, Misha wandered up and down the hallways, in and out of student rooms. A few rooms were still occupied, and every student she found offered Misha a goodie. At the end of the building was a shower room. Misha stepped carefully across the tiled floor, fiddling with the wet towels and shampoo bottles as she went. I turned on one of the shower nozzles and Misha drank from it.

We put Misha on the freight elevator and rode her to the third floor, where a french-fry party was in full swing at the end of the hall. Misha headed straight for the party. Five deep-fat fryers were stuffed full of potatoes bubbling in hot grease. French fries on paper-towel-lined plates were all over the room. A few girls rushed over and fed Misha ketchup-dipped fried potatoes while others tied helium-filled Happy Graduation balloons to her tail and halter. The blonde who'd met us outside and invited us into the dorm draped silk scarves and plastic Hawaiian leis around Misha's neck. Then several of the graduates gave me their cameras and asked me to take pictures of them as they gathered around Misha in a tight circle.

The seniors were giddy yet sad. A big part of their lives was over and their new adult phases were about to begin. With Misha around, they acted like little girls in women's bodies. I was glad we could help make their last days at school memorable.

Stuffed full of french fries, Misha said goodbye to the seniors and I wished them good luck. They all said, "We'll never forget your horse. We've been watching her outside our windows through midterms and finals, first-job rejections, and lousy dates. She's been part of our college experience. Thanks for letting her come into our dorm."

During the winter months, Misha and I didn't see anybody when we walked to the college or while we rested in the campus woods. To liven up our experience, we'd stop at the local IGA grocery located a half mile away from the campus. I'd tie Misha to a tree on the outskirts of the parking lot and hurry inside the store to buy a box of graham crackers or a bag of carrots for her and a big two-liter bottle of diet pop for me. Because I worried about Misha being outside the store all alone, I tried to use the express checkout lane. Sometimes when the checkouts were all jammed and busy, I'd ask the person in line ahead of me if I could please go first, explaining that my horse was tied up to a tree. People were always quite generous in letting me cut in ahead of them.

Every once in a while, Misha acted cranky when we finally got to the campus or the grocery. Maybe she was uneasy about being so far from home, or perhaps I'd walked her too far and overtired her. On those rare occasions, I telephoned Mark and asked him to come pick us up in the Nickel's truck.

As soon as Misha heard her truck rumble onto the campus, she'd wail and whinny, buck and kick, and race around in circles until Mark got to her. Then she'd slather him with kisses.

But I hated to make Mark stop in the middle of whatever he was doing to come get us, so most of the time Misha and I hoofed it home on our own steam. On our way back, I usually jogged the first four and a half miles and rode Misha the second four and a half. Sometimes I'd make the mistake of stopping at the college library to pick up a few books before we left. Then I'd have to lug them the whole way under my arm. On the way back, we never stopped to visit horses, dogs, students, or Mr. Pitts, because we were both in a hurry to get home. I longed for a hot bath and dry socks. Misha craved warmth, quiet, and corn.

A year after we started our triathlons, Misha weighed in at a mere 1,320 pounds and had an eighty-one-inch waist. I weighed in at 127. She'd lost 110 pounds. I'd lost one pound. I hadn't gotten smaller. In fact, my shoe size grew from a 6 1/2 to a 7. Too much weight pushing down on my feet, I guessed.

Even though I never found out what it would be like to be skinny, Misha slimmed down and never regained her weight after our year of endurance walking. We still put her on the scale twice a year. Nowadays, the grain employees always yell out, "1,320 pounds."

After all those miles, I'm glad to know at least one of us lost weight.

Chapter Eleven

I'd tried to give Misha everything I thought she'd ever need to be happy. Over the years, I had convinced myself she was content with her lot in life. Then I began noticing how she would linger longer and not want to leave when we passed other horses. That made me wonder if she was lonely. Maybe she wasn't as happy as she deserved to be.

Misha had always enjoyed stopping to kibbutz over the fence with the mares and geldings in our neighborhood. If I was riding her, I'd lay across her back and rest while she grazed and visited with the Mourers' Belgian twins or the Lucas's herd of standardbreds. If we were jogging together, I'd drop her lead and prop myself against a tree while she nickered and nudged the Olivers' Morgan yearling.

Then suddenly, her needs seemed to change.

I began to notice her increased interest in the neighborhood horses, especially the males. She seemed to be yearning for horse companionship. Maybe having me for her best friend wasn't good enough after all.

When I broached the subject with Mark, he was adamant. "Absolutely not. No way we are getting another horse. You know what will happen? The second horse will end up living inside. Then I'll have to walk around two horses when I want to wash my hands at the kitchen sink."

"But I'm worried she's lonely."

"How can she be lonely? You're with her almost every hour of the day. Besides, she has Mouse and the deer in the yard and you take her to visit the neighborhood horses all the time," he said.

This wasn't the first time I had talked to Mark about a second horse. Years before, word had spread throughout the hospital about how Misha lived in the house with me, and on many occasions I'd show up for work to find some nurse I'd never met waiting for me at the ICU doors.

"Are you Jackie Tresl?" she'd ask.

"Yes . . ."

"You don't know me but I have a fifteen-year-old gelding that I desperately need to find a home for." Then the nurse would proceed to tell me some sad tale about why she was going to have to sell her horse to the meatpackers if I couldn't take it. I was always everyone's last resort. "I've heard about how good you are to your mare and I was hoping you'd adopt my horse and love it just as much."

I could have had forty unwanted horses if I'd have agreed to take them in. They were all beautiful, healthy animals, offered to me free of charge. Some owners tried to sweeten the deal by throwing in a saddle or a winter's worth of hay. But back then, I believed Misha loved being an only horse and didn't want to share my attentions or affections with another.

It was around her sixth birthday that I began questioning my judgment. Maybe she did want and need her own horse buddy.

Ten miles away lived a twenty-year-old gelding named Rusty. He was Misha's and my favorite horse in the whole township. Quiet, polite, dignified, smart—he was everything anyone could ever want in a horse. He spent his life in a 100-acre field with plenty of hay to eat and three mares to keep him company. No one rode him much anymore and that suited him just fine.

I thought Rusty would be the perfect friend for Misha. With him in the yard, she'd probably stay outside more. My mother had often accused me of imposing my will on Misha by forcing her to act more like a person than a horse. If Rusty came to live with us, maybe Misha would be more mare-ly, more in touch with her authentic equine self.

I asked Rusty's owners if I could borrow him. "Just for a little while? I think Misha may be lonely and in need of company. I don't want to adopt a horse only to find out I've made a mistake. I'd like Rusty to be my trial horse to see how Misha reacts."

Rusty's owners gave me a queer look but, in an attempt to be neighborly, they said I could take him for as long as I wanted. Mark drove over to pick him up in the Nickel's truck for me. I made Misha stay at home and wait. It took us a long time to load Rusty because he was used to riding in stock trailers, but eventually he figured out how to walk up the ramp. Mark buckled him in and we drove off.

Misha was standing at the gate waiting for us. We pulled down into the yard and let Rusty out of the truck. Misha glanced over at him and kept grazing. "I'm surprised she's so nonchalant. I figured the second Rusty was in her territory, Misha would be prancing around in circles," I said.

Mark pulled the truck into the barn and went back to his farm chores. I sat in the pasture and watched Misha and Rusty for an hour. They eyed each other warily but both concentrated on eating. Convinced they were getting along okay, I went into the house to make supper. Within minutes, Misha pushed through the door to settle herself beside me in the kitchen. A half an hour later when I went out to check on Rusty, I found him sleeping against the house with his rump pressed up against the porch door. Misha saw him, stuck her nose out the door, and gave him a churlish nudge.

The next day they grazed side by side. Wherever Misha went, Rusty followed. I said, "See that, I was right, Misha was lonely. Look how she stays with Rusty."

"I think you've got that backwards. Rusty is the one hanging onto Misha. She acts like she wants to be alone," Mark said.

Misha stayed out grazing longer than usual that day. Around suppertime she sauntered into the kitchen. Five minutes later, Rusty followed and took his customary nap by the porch door. Misha went out later in the evening for a few bites of hay. Rusty stayed close beside her. When she was full, she walked back into the kitchen. I noticed Rusty standing nearby, carefully watching how she opened her door to come inside the house.

Rusty discovered Nickel's Thrift Bakery treats on his second day with us. The first raspberry jelly doughnut I fed him made him smile. I shared all of Misha's treats with him. In ten hours I went through two dozen chocolate crullers, a loaf of cinnamon raisin bread, and six cherry lunchbox pies.

The third morning, Misha and Rusty grazed together. At noon, Misha walked through the porch door into the kitchen. I was busy praising her for coming in when suddenly I heard the porch door bang open again. Rusty had let himself in and was standing on Misha's porch. He settled himself in against the couch and fell asleep. Rusty standing on the porch behind her bothered Misha, but as soon as she started helping me fry up the potato pancakes, she forgot he was there.

Mark came in for lunch and said, "I knew it. I told you this would happen. Now I've got two horses in the house."

By the fourth day, Misha would hardly leave the kitchen. Rusty didn't want to get off of the porch unless Misha was with him so both of them were inside most of the day. Sometimes Rusty would try to stick his nose through the doorway into the kitchen. As soon as Misha felt his hot breath on her rump, she'd twirl around and nip him. As far as she was concerned, Rusty had to stay on the porch. She didn't want him to put even one of his nostril whiskers into her kitchen space.

I didn't know if I could count on Rusty not to do his business on Misha's porch. It wouldn't have been fair to Misha if I let him make a mess in her "bedroom." So, to be safe, I walked Rusty out into the yard every few hours.

On day five, Misha tried to tell me she'd had enough. When they walked outside to graze, Misha kicked Rusty. He insisted on following her even after she stuck her hoof in his face. She couldn't get rid of him. She'd race away and hide in the kitchen, but within seconds, Rusty would be standing behind her on the porch. When I tried to lock him out, he butted his nose into the porch window screen until the screen came out of its tracks and fell on the floor. Then he stuck his whole head and neck through the opening and called for Misha.

She didn't want any part of him on her porch. When she charged out to scare him away, she trampled the screen. Just then Mark came and said, "Why are you letting these horses rip up our screens?"

Before I could explain, Mark announced that borrowing Rusty had been a mistake and he thought it was time for us to truck him back to the neighbors. I begged for one last chance.

In the afternoon, I put halters on Misha and Rusty and tied a clothesline to Rusty's noseband. I hopped on Misha and ponied Rusty beside us. I took them out into the wide-open fields, thinking if they used up some of their mischievous energy riding side by side, they might get along better.

Misha had always been the perfect mount. I'd never had one dangerous moment on her back. But the day I towed Rusty along with us, she went wild. She stood on her back legs, turned her hind end towards him and urinated all over his face and neck. I tried hard to hold on while she kicked him and took off towards home. I let go of his clothesline to avoid more injury, but Rusty was smitten and in love. He ran to catch up with Misha and then stayed right behind her.

In an effort to separate them, I leapt off of Misha and stuck her in the barn. When Rusty lost sight of her, he bolted down the road in a panic, his clothesline trailing behind him. While I set off running after Rusty, Misha whinnied and shrieked from inside the barn because I'd abandoned her. I yelled for Mark as loud as I could, hoping he'd hear me and come to my rescue. Five minutes later, I saw him driving towards me on his tractor.

He caught Rusty and put him back in the yard. I walked Misha home and put her in the kitchen. Mark told me to get Rusty loaded into the bakery truck. "Misha doesn't want another horse in her yard. I want him out of here before she hurts him," he said.

Rusty hated to go. He wasn't afraid to load; he just didn't want to leave. I tried several times to walk him onto the ramp, but he resisted. Finally, I gave up coaxing him and dug out a day-old Nickel's Thrift chocolate birthday cake from the freezer instead. I stuck the whole cake into the front of the truck. Rusty smelled the chocolate and couldn't resist. He was in the truck and gobbling up the cake just as Mark climbed into the driver's seat. I took half of the cake away from Rusty, saving the rest for later.

Rusty didn't seem happy to be home. We put him in his field and he ignored the mares. He hung his head over my shoulder and nickered when Mark came to say goodbye. It was hard to leave him because he didn't want to be left. I'd grown accustomed to him snoozing on the porch.

"C'mon now," Mark said, "it's time to get back to Misha."

I kissed Rusty's nose and laid the rest of the chocolate birthday cake at his feet. The last thing I saw as we drove away was Rusty licking white icing and brown crumbs off his lips.

Misha did not act surprised when we arrived home without Rusty. I got the impression she was muttering under her breath, "It's about time you got rid of him." She was concerned when she smelled chocolate cake on my hands and I wasn't forthcoming in offering any to her. So before I settled into my reading chair, I gave her some of those Hostess chocolate cupcakes with the squiggle of white icing along the top. That satisfied her and while I read, she slept, happy not to have Rusty on her porch.

I figured if Misha couldn't adjust to having polite, quiet Rusty on her farm, she probably wouldn't be happy with any horse I would adopt for her. I decided Mark was right. Misha wasn't lonely for equine companionship. I was company enough.

So when our friends Tim and Jessica invited Mark, Misha, and me down to their 2,000-acre farm to horseback ride one weekend, I couldn't imagine how Misha would react to three other horses walking and trotting along with her. I told Jessica that I'd always ridden Misha alone, never with other horses. Jessica said this would be a great opportunity for Misha to develop better social skills and that if she misbehaved, she and I could stay back at the end of the line.

Mark hardly ever rode Misha. She was a one-person horse and responded favorably only to my cues. She listened to and obeyed Mark as long as he was standing on the ground beside her. But if he got onto her back, she fussed and walked slower than an arthritic octogenarian crossing a busy Manhattan street. Jessica said she'd lend Mark a horse to ride, since we only had Misha.

Mouse was fifteen years old by then. He was deaf and nearly blind, thin and weak. His epilepsy had returned six months earlier. He averaged two seizures a week. He'd only eat if I fed him out of my hand and he'd only take his medicine after half an hour of coaxing. I couldn't leave him alone and no one else could care for him, so he came with us. I gathered his favorite, broken up, plastic yellow litter box, his anti-seizure pills, an emergency syringe of Valium in case of status epilepticus, several jars of baby food (most days that's all he could swallow) and Misha's horse blanket because he loved to sleep on it.

We loaded Misha, Mouse, and all their assorted accessories into the Nickel's truck and drove three hours to Tim and Jessica's. Mouse slept on my lap the entire trip and, as soon as we arrived, I settled him on Misha's blanket in the corner of Jessica's living room. While Mark visited with Tim and inspected Tim's bulldozer, backhoe, and new Ford tractor, I jumped on top of Misha and rode her around the yard so she could meet the many horses and adjust to the new surroundings.

Jessica's father is a veterinarian who specializes in horses. Because Jessica is so good-hearted, she winds up adopting a lot of animals whose owners, for one reason or another, can't keep them any more. At the time of our visit, Jessica had sixteen horses, thirty rabbits, fifty pigeons, twenty-three chickens, five dogs, three cats, and a domestic tom turkey named Napoleon. Any time anyone tells Jessica his pet is going to be put to sleep, Jessica offers to adopt it.

So Misha had a lot to see. She sniffed the horse corral, the dog kennels, the rabbit hutches and the pigeon aviary. I trotted her across the hay fields and into the woods. Once she had used up her nervous energy, I rode her back to Jessica's yard, and let her loose so she could rest and graze. The other horses were in a fenced-in field at least a quarter mile away from her.

It took a long time for Tim and Jessica to get three horses saddled up and ready to ride. The horses had to be caught, the dirt on their backs brushed off, the bridles and bits fitted onto heads, the saddle pads fluffed up, stirrups adjusted, cinch straps tightened and riding helmets donned. Forty-five minutes later, the three horses were finally ready to go. No wonder I rode bareback.

Tim led us out onto the wooded trail. Jessica rode behind Tim, Mark behind Jessica, and Misha brought up the end of the line. Jessica's horses had been over the trail hundreds of times, so they had the terrain memorized. For Misha, every stream, slope, and boulder was mildly spooky. But she fearlessly jumped, waded, and cantered along without a moment's hesitation.

At the ten-mile mark, Tim stopped our posse for a rest. The three other horses sipped river water through their bits. Misha stayed downstream, off to the sidelines, not wanting to get too close. If one of the horses moved towards her, she backed us away, trying to isolate herself and me from the group.

Tim turned us around towards home, saying we'd ride the entire fifty-mile trail tomorrow. As soon as we got back, Jessica removed the saddles and turned her horses out while I grabbed a box of graham crackers for Misha's reward. Then I went from horse to horse and offered a handful to all. Sixteen horses can demolish a box of graham crackers in no time.

Jessica had given the four of us permission to sleep in their family room. Mark, Mouse, and I were going to bed down on the foldout couch and Misha would lie down on the floor beside us.

I got up at 3 A.M. and walked Misha outside to do her business. At 5:30 A.M., Jessica's three roosters woke us after crowing at the rising sun. Misha had slept poorly, but she was up and ready for the fifty-mile ride.

The trail was beautiful as it meandered deep into untouched valleys and vistas of the southern Ohio rolling hills. Tim led. Misha carried up the rear. When we had ridden for three hours, we stopped beside a gurgling stream. The horses sipped water. I took off my shoes and socks and dipped my feet in. Misha stood guard over me.

We were heading back to Jessica's house when we crossed over the ten-mile trail we had ridden yesterday. It didn't look familiar to me but Tim said we'd been over it the day before. Misha started to act agitated and was sucking in big gulps of air. She tried to pass the horses in front of her. But the path was narrow and she couldn't help but brush up against them when she pushed by. She kept rushing up, then stopping and lagging behind when she saw that she didn't have enough room to pass. Finally I asked the group if they could stop so Misha could zoom by.

As soon as the three horses moved over, Misha took off. She lowered her head and galloped. She had never moved so fast. When

I looked behind me, Mark and the others were already out of sight. All I could do was hold on tight. This time, Misha was in charge. Before I had time to wonder where the heck we were going, Misha delivered us to Jessica's house.

She was out of breath but very relieved to be rid of the other horses. She nudged me towards the truck. I gave her some carrots and wiped her face with a damp washcloth. I changed into dry pants. An hour later, Tim, Jessica, and Mark showed up.

Jessica said, "That's a pretty smart horse you've got there. She remembered the trail after only one trip. She sure was in a hurry to get back. She wants to have you all to herself."

"Is that what this was all about?" I asked. "I couldn't figure out what was going on. I just held on and let her go."

"Looks to me like Misha doesn't like other horses," Jessica said. "She's a loner."

When we got back home, Misha didn't want to do anything but sleep and eat Nickel's desserts. A week passed before I rode her again. This time she didn't slow down when we passed the Lucas's standardbreds and she didn't whinny back when the Morgan called to her. She had played with horses and shared her home with a gelding. Those experiences convinced her she was better off sticking with me. I was companion enough for her.

Chapter Twelve

hen we moved to southeastern Ohio in 1984, we
bought a 25-acre parcel out of a larger 500-acre farm.
We were born and raised in the suburbs, so our 5
acres of pasture and 20 acres of mixed deciduous woods seemed like
a lot of land to us. We saved our money and hoped that one day in
the future we might buy another adjoining parcel. Back then, Tom
Colson, the farmer who owned the rest of the land, wasn't interested
in selling, which was lucky for us because we couldn't afford to buy
it.

In 1991, Mr. Colson's wife got sick and he was forced to auction
off 300 acres to cover the exorbitant cost of her hospitalization. In
1993, she died. Not long after, Mr. Colson married a woman from
Atlanta and decided to sell his house, barn, and the 206 acres he
had left. It was a spectacular farm with lots of local agricultural ap-
peal, but the land languished on the market.

Mr. Colson waited a year for someone to make him a fair offer.
He and his new wife were gradually losing hope, afraid their farm
might never sell. Desperate to move to Georgia, they called a local
land broker. In southern Ohio, land brokers are men who buy up big
farms, usually from retired, aging farmers. They split the hundreds of
acres into 5- and 10-acre parcels and resell the small tracts to city

dwellers, who use the land mostly on holidays and weekends. Sectioning up big farms is bad for rural communities because the farms are lost forever. The cost of the land skyrockets once property is divided. If a person took a hankering to buy back enough acres to reestablish one large farm, he'd have to have a million dollars to spend.

When we found out that a land broker was visiting Mr. Colson, we got scared. If Mr. Colson's 206 acres were sectioned into 10-acre lots, we'd have at least twenty new neighbors. Divided into 5-acre lots, we'd have at least forty. Our quiet way of life would be gone forever. Either we'd have to adjust to a busy, bustling neighborhood up and down our dirt road or we'd have to move. Neither option sounded attractive.

Mr. Colson wanted $175,000 for the farm. We had $80,000 in the bank. Mark met with him and offered $120,000, saying we'd try to get a loan for the rest. Mr. Colson called Mark's offer an "insult bid" and rejected it.

A few months passed. An out-of-town veal producer heard about Colson's farm and rushed in with an offer to buy. Mr. Colson got ready to move. He and his new bride packed up their furniture and clothes and, assuming the farm was sold, they left for Atlanta. Mr. Colson had just signed a lease for his new apartment when the bank called. The loan officer told Mr. Colson their bank was refusing to finance the cost of another Ohio veal operation. The deal fell through.

Our neighbor stopped over and told us about the bank turning down the loan for Mr. Colson's farm. I took the news as an omen and called Mr. Colson's realtor. She agreed to meet with us an hour later. It was 10 P.M. when we signed the papers that said we were officially offering Mr. Colson $135,000 for his farm. "That's all we have. We can't come up with a penny more."

The next morning the realtor drove to our house to tell us we'd just bought ourselves another house, barn, and 206 acres. We were overjoyed until reality set in. Where were we going to get the rest of the money?

I called my mother. I told her what had happened and that I knew nothing about taking out a loan. I needed her to tell me which banks charged the cheapest rates of interest.

My mother said, "You know, sweetie, someday I might like to retire down there next to you and since that farm has such a nice house on it, how about I give you the rest of the money to pay off the farm?"

That was the closest I ever came to fainting. "But Mom, you don't have that kind of money to hand over to me."

"Yes I do. I have a nice little nest egg put away. Besides, I'll rest better knowing I have a house in the country all ready and waiting for me when I want it."

The next day, true to her word, she sent off a check for $55,000 to us. By the end of the month the paperwork was signed, the real estate transfer was made, and the deed was ours. The first thing we did when we got home from the registrar's office was to walk Misha over her new farm. She was duly impressed with our purchase.

It was two years before Mark got caught up on all that had to be done on the farm. Fences needed repair, trees that had fallen in the hayfields had to be removed, brambles and weed trees needed to be cut, cattails had to be cleared from the edge of the pond, and a complete interior and exterior paint job had to be done before we could rent out the house. The barn roof leaked, the septic tank was plugged, and several old gas lines seeped.

We rolled up our sleeves and got to work. Misha followed us everywhere we went. We'd spend one day working on the pond, another at the edge of the woods, the next in a thicket of wild raspberries. I didn't ever have to put Misha on a lead. As soon as I called for her, she'd run out of the gate and tag close on my heels. Mark and

I would settle into whatever farm chore we were doing and she'd keep an eye on us and graze nearby. Even when we were deep in the woods and there was no grass, Misha would stay at our sides, nibbling at mosses, ferns, and scrawny maple branches. Wherever we went, she always found something delicious to eat.

When I painted the inside of the rental house, Misha painted with me. If I was in the master bedroom, so was she. The bathroom was too small for her to fit, so she stood on the threshold with her head dangling over the commode. The living room was her favorite because it had an enormous picture window overlooking the hayfields. She'd stand with her nose against the glass watching the few cars that drove by, or the deer that leapt past. People would stop their cars and point at the window when they saw Misha peering out at them.

At the end of every painting day, Misha came out of the house with white or beige paint on some part of her face, tail, or rump. No matter how often I pushed her away from the wet walls or paint roller tray, she always managed to get some on her. One hot and humid morning, I filled up the paint pan and was laying some dropcloths when Misha stuck her nose down the back of my shirt. I was grouchy because I had been painting nonstop for six days in a row. "Would you PLEASE leave me alone!" I shouted.

Misha's lower lip quivered. She took two steps back, acting as if I'd smacked her with a searing cast-iron skillet. I stood up and wrapped my arms around her neck. "I'm sorry I yelled, Misha. I'm so tired of painting and it's so hot."

She licked my face and followed me back over to the paint bucket. I had just lathered my brush with paint when I heard the sound of something wet striking the wall. Misha had dipped the end of her tail into the bucket and was smacking her beige paint-laden tail against the wall.

I sat back on the floor and laughed.

I took her outside and hosed her off. Then we went home for an

117

ice cream break. Each of us gobbled up a bowl of orange sherbet before going back to paint.

The rental house kitchen intrigued Misha because it contained a stove and a refrigerator, appliances she associated with food. The first time she stuck her head into the empty oven, she was disappointed not to find any baking cookies or pies. After that, she didn't even bother checking out the fridge. Way in the back of one of the cupboards, I found an old box of cereal, which kept her busy for a few minutes. But mostly Misha slept while I painted the inside walls and Mark scraped the exterior.

Our final chore in readying the house for renting was scrubbing the rugs. Every room, even the kitchen, had wall-to-wall carpeting. Misha wasn't allowed back inside the house once the rugs were clean, so she hovered around outside the doors and tried to sneak in every time I came in and out. She did succeed once in getting both front feet into the kitchen foyer before I could stop her. I had to re-scrub the foyer rug.

Misha loved helping us interview prospective renters. We ran ads in the local newspapers and, being first-time landlords, we let anyone who was interested come out for the grand tour. At least twenty-five families, lots of them with little kids, showed up. With each arrival, I'd have to push Misha away from the door so they could get inside.

Children loved to lag behind their parents and stay in the kitchen to watch Misha. As soon as the adults were busy touring the bedrooms and bathroom, the children would open the kitchen door so Misha could burst in. I'd come around the corner and find her standing with muddy hooves in the living room, looking out of the big picture window, while the children giggled and hooted with delight. I had to hand-scrub sections of the kitchen and living-room rugs three more times.

But I couldn't complain. Misha was an icebreaker around strangers. She put everyone at ease, especially me. When I first started showing the house, I was nervous. Then Misha would stick her head inside the kitchen window to eye up a prospective renter or rattle the doorknobs to get their attention and everyone would laugh and tell me what a beautiful, smart horse I had. Misha knew they were complimenting her, so she hammed it up even more, which relaxed us all.

It took Misha more than a month to understand that the house was now rented and she had to stay away. She was no longer allowed to traipse up onto the tenants' lawn or try to sneak into their kitchen. One day I couldn't find her at home in her yard, so I marched up to the rental house. There she was, chewing up the renters' freshly planted tomatoes and green peppers. When I ran over to catch her, she slipped around the back and dashed in between the clean laundry hanging on the clothesline. Earlier in the day she had rolled in the mud and so she managed to soil several of the white undershirts and blouses.

But everyone always forgave Misha her mischievousness. She had so much fun doing whatever she was doing that her enthusiasm was contagious. It was hard to be angry with her. I bought new vegetable plants to replace the ones Misha had eaten, and two giant-sized jugs of detergent and bleach. I walked up to the rental house and offered them as an apology. The renters told me my gestures were unnecessary, but appreciated. "Having Misha running around our house is lots more fun than aggravation. And my kids love her," the wife said.

Even so, I had to scold Misha. I did not want her bothering the renters. She must have understood my message because after that, she never sneaked up there again. The next time she went up, it was because we had to repaint the house and find new renters again.

Misha's life changed dramatically after we bought the additional 206 acres. Imagine being a grass-gobbling, wide-open-space-loving horse whose farm has suddenly grown almost ten times bigger. Misha loved to race from pasture to pasture, nibbling here, tasting there, sampling and testing to find out whether orchard grass was better than the timothy, or hop's clover sweeter than the red and white varieties.

For nearly two years, I stopped riding Misha on the dirt roads. Instead, I used paths that Mark and I made on our land. I designed a course of a mile and a quarter that wound through our pastures and the edges of our woods. Before I rode her over any of it, I marked the path with stakes and walked every inch of it, filling in woodchuck holes and moving big rocks. Holes in a horse's field can be deadly. If a trotting horse steps into a deep hole, he'll probably break his leg. Depending on the type of fracture, the broken leg bone may not be mendable. Not all fractures can be successfully set into a cast and for those that can, the orthopedic procedure may cost thousands of dollars. Usually, when a horse breaks his leg, he is euthanized. So I had to be absolutely sure that there were no dangerous holes on Misha's riding path.

Meanwhile, Mark was busy reopening fifty-year-old logging roads that wound through our woods. With his tractor and chainsaw, he removed fallen trees and cleared paths so Misha and I could ride and hike over them. When he was finished, I grabbed the hedge clippers and climbed onto Misha's back. As she rode me over the logging paths, I cut off all the low-hanging branches that would hit me in the head unless I ducked. It took me hours to get them all clipped back, but it was worth it because I hate getting smacked in the face by a tree limb when I'm riding.

Our hard work paid off. Misha rode faster, harder, and with more gusto than ever. She loved perambulating over the farm and didn't miss the road pebbles, the cars, or even the neighborhood horses.

Mark bought a secondhand New Holland square baler (circa 1934) and started making our own hay. Because we could only feed second-cutting to Misha, we had lots of first-cutting bales to sell. Within a year, Mark had paid for his baler from all the bales he'd sold. Misha always came along with us when we cut, raked, and baled hay. She never wanted to be left out of our activities.

While Mark mowed the edges of the field, Misha grazed in the center. When the cutter got near the middle, she moved to the edges and ate the grass Mark had just cut. While we raked the hay, Misha ran from row to row, trampling the fluffed dry hay under her feet and stealing snatches from every pile. Then she followed behind the hay baler and ripped out samples from almost every bale that popped out. Mark would yell and tell her not to get so close to the machinery. She'd listen and back off for five minutes. But she had appointed herself The Official Hay Taste-Tester and no one, not even her "father," was going to interfere with her most important job.

My favorite place on our land—what I call the jewel of our farm—is our quarter-acre pond, which had been neglected for years. The cattails had taken over and the shoreline had shrunk, and rejuvenating it was our top priority. Misha trotted behind the tractor as we headed for the pond. As soon as we were parked, she'd walk to the edge and splash the edge of the water with her hooves and nose. When we yanked cattails out with a big scoop that we dragged on the back of the tractor, Misha ate them. She loved the cattail roots, and sometimes I'd have to push her away from the pond for fear she'd eat too many.

We worked on the pond several hours a day for two weeks, and at the end of our workdays, we always took a family swim. Misha wouldn't walk into the pond unless we guided her in on her lead. But the minute her tummy touched the water, she dog-paddled, bobbed, splashed, and nudged Mark along as he floated inside his inner tube. Misha loved to swim if we swam with her.

When visitors came, we took them to the pond. If it was summer, we invited them to swim. Once our company was busy swimming, I'd stand Misha in four-foot-deep water and hop onto her back. There I'd sit, like a regal lifeguard on my satin horsechair, watching while everyone else swam. Misha never fussed. She'd hold me up for hours, standing still and restful, while kids and adults flailed wet arms, legs, rafts, and rubber toys around her.

When we bought the farm, the pond was full of tiny, hungry bluegills with bulgy eyes. My county agricultural extension agent said protruding eyeballs were symptoms of starved fish. I said, "You mean our poor fish are suffering?"

"They probably are. Your only solution is to fish them hard. Try to catch all the small ones you can. Then throw them on the bank and let them die. You've got to get them out of there. They're no good for your pond's ecosystem," he explained.

"You mean because the fish are hungry, I'm supposed to yank them out by their mouths on a hook and heave them into the grass to die?" I asked.

"Yep. That's what you have to do."

That didn't make any sense to me. It seemed more logical just to feed them. So the next time I went to the Nickel's Thrift Bakery, I asked the clerk for some old, unwanted bread. She told me to come back on Sunday and she'd fill up the back of our truck with bread at a price we could afford.

Two days later, Mark drove the truck in and the bakery lady gave us 200 loaves of bread and 500 hot-dog buns for five dollars. When we got home, I laid screens out in the sunshine and spread the bread and buns on the screens to dry. The next day, I packed the crispy dried bread into trash bags and stored the bags in two clean garbage cans. The bread would have gotten moldy if I hadn't processed and stored it away. Plus, I could crumble it into tiny, bluegill-sized bites.

Once I had a hefty stash of bread, Misha and I went to the pond to feed the fish every other day. When the weather was warm, I walked her into belly-high water and let her watch me while I flung out bread. She soon decided that the fish should have to share, and she began begging for her cut. I wouldn't give her but a few slices, so she took matters into her own hooves and started snatching the bread out of the water while the fish were busy eating it.

Even though I scolded her, she persisted. Then one day she scooped up a piece of bread and got a mouthful of bluegill. The fish flopped around on her tongue and its spiny fins cut her lips. Instead of spitting it out, she bit down and tasted raw fish. A look of pure disgust crossed her face. That didn't stop her, though. She still tried to steal the bread. But she learned to grab at the water daintily. If a bluegill happened into her mouth, she let go of the bread to let the fish drop out of her mouth.

We stopped going to Salt Fork to swim once we had our own pond. There was so much litter on the public beaches that it wasn't safe to take her anymore. Our beach was clean, mowed, and familiar, plus we didn't have to drive to get there. And even though it was small, our pond was plenty big enough to swim around in. In the winter, our bluegills lost their appetites. When I threw bread in for them, they swam up and looked at it. A few took a nibble or two, but usually everything I offered them fell to the bottom of the pond. They didn't get hungry again until March.

Even though Misha and I didn't have fish to feed in the winter, we went to the pond almost every day. When the water was frozen solid, I'd put a heavy blanket on her, grab my ice skates, and ride her over to the pond. I'd let her loose to graze while I spent an hour speed-racing in broad circles around the ice. At first, Misha would try to follow me around from one side of the pond to the other, but she quickly understood that no matter where she positioned herself, I'd be skating away from her and then skating right back.

Though the grass around the pond was stiff and frozen, Misha found plenty to eat. She was never in a hurry to go home, even if it was only ten degrees out. Her blanket kept her warm and she enjoyed getting away from the kitchen to spend some quality time with me, even with a windchill of twenty-two degrees below zero.

I'd skate until my clothes were soaked with perspiration, then slip on my shoes and hop on Misha. It would have been an uncomfortable walk home with the cold wind on my damp skin, my skate blades banging into my frozen arms, my ankles sore from skating, and me all worn out and tired. Being able to ride Misha instead was a luxury, like having a warm, chauffeured limousine waiting for me.

Sometimes when we found ourselves in the middle of a prolonged cold spell, the only times Misha and I ventured outside together were to skate. Like Arctic explorers, we pushed through the ice and snow to make memories. Our relationship is the strongest and closest during the long, dark winter months when Misha depends on me almost exclusively for her entertainment.

In 1993, our lives changed. After we bought our extra 206 acres, we stayed on the farm to enjoy it. We semiretired the Nickel's Bakery truck and swam and rode in our own back yard. We put up forty bluebird boxes and three wood-duck boxes, and created ruffed grouse and turkey habitat. Our outward focus shifted inward, and Misha became a stay-at-home horse. Our traveling days were over.

Chapter Thirteen

In 1994, Mouse turned sixteen years old. His health had
been poor for four years and had been rapidly failing for the
past nine months. His seizures were more frequent and lasted
longer. An abscessed tooth caused the right side of his face to swell
up. And unless Mark kept the temperature in the house at seventy-
eight degrees or warmer, Mouse would shiver uncontrollably. I was
at a crossroads; should I continue his aggressive medical treatment
or have him put to sleep?

As far as I could tell, Mouse wasn't in much pain. When his
joints looked stiff, I'd slip him a sliver of aspirin. He spent most of
his life sleeping on Misha's horse blanket. He walked to his litter
box four or five times a day and curled up in my lap for at least an
hour every evening, but other than that, he didn't move around
much. I hand-fed him baby food and toothpick-sized pieces of
lunchmeat and kept his water bowl filled and set next to Misha's
blanket.

When Mouse's face swelled up, the vet gave him an injection of
ampicillin and a steroid and cautioned me that the medicine would
probably not cure Mouse's abscessed tooth. "You may have to consider surgery. And, since he's sixteen years old and very frail, I have
to warn you, the anesthesia may kill him."

The shot helped Mouse for two days. On the third day, his face puffed more and he couldn't swallow, eat, or drink. I knew his bad tooth needed to be pulled. I asked Mark if he thought I should put Mouse through the surgery, considering that it might kill him.

"He'll die if he *doesn't* have the surgery, won't he?" Mark asked.

"Yes."

"Then what do you have to lose? Take the chance, pay for the surgery, see how he does. Mouse is worth every penny. He's been with us since before we got married."

The next morning, I sat in the waiting room while Mouse was anesthetized and prepped in the pet operating room. Not long after, the vet came out to tell me every tooth Mouse had left in his mouth was rotten and all of them had to be pulled. I said, "Do whatever you think is best."

Forty-five minutes later, the vet had good news. "Your cat did very well. We were right to pull that abscessed tooth. It had to come out. Antibiotics would have never cured his underlying infection. Mouse is still asleep, but I thought you might like to see him."

I followed the vet back into the surgical suite. Mouse had a tiny endotracheal tube sticking out of his mouth and an IV line inserted in his front leg. He was unresponsive, but breathing, so I was reassured. I thanked the vet and asked him when I could take Mouse home.

He said, "How about three hours?"

I said, "How about one?"

He said, "How about we split the difference? Come back in two hours and he's all yours."

I was grateful for the terrific job the vet and his staff had done, so while I waited for Mouse to recover, I spent the two hours making dozens of chocolate chip cookies as a thank-you gift. I drove to the clinic, paid my bill, gave the staff their cookies, and carried my limp, cold cat to my car.

126

As soon as I got Mouse home, I laid him in a cushioned box and let him sleep. Misha came in and sniffed the air, which was filled with the smell of betadine, alcohol, and blood. She followed the scent over to Mouse's box and stood guard over him for the next five hours while Mouse lay motionless and unaware. A lot of blood drained from his mouth onto the bedding in his box, so I frequently lifted up his head and put a fresh towel under it. I repositioned him every hour by flipping him over onto his other side.

When Mouse finally woke up, he was famished. I fed him two jars of baby food and a bowl of milk. I helped him to the litter pan and put him back in his box. But he refused to sleep any more. Instead, he began wandering around the house in an agitated, dazed state. No matter how many times I tried to hold him or soothe him, he wouldn't settle. So I gave up and let him roam.

While he strolled around the house, blood dripped from his mouth. Misha smelled his blood, saw him stumbling around and grew concerned. I tried to make Misha go outside so she wouldn't have to witness Mouse's pain and suffering, but she wouldn't leave. She followed Mouse around, watching every move he made.

Usually, Misha wasn't allowed to walk through the house because when she did, she fiddled with the books, the TV, the electronic equipment, and the electrical cords. But on the day of Mouse's surgery, Misha wasn't interested in anything but him. I was worried he might get under her feet and she would accidentally step on him, but my fears were unfounded. Misha was gentle and slow. When Mouse curled up against Misha's hooves, he seemed comforted. He didn't mind when she licked the blood off his fur and his face. Misha had never paid much attention to Mouse before his surgery. Except for being careful not to step on him, she had always ignored him. But after his surgery, Misha acted protective and nurturing towards him.

When Mouse recovered, he was healthier than he'd been in a

long time. His seizures tapered off to one every few weeks, and he ate cat food out of a bowl on his own. When Misha was in the kitchen, Mouse often wandered over and cuddled up close to her. He was still deaf and blind, although I believe he could make out shapes in the dark. He even gained two pounds. I began having hope Mouse might rally and have a few good years before he died.

Misha continued to hover. One night Mouse had a terrible and long-lasting seizure as Misha was leaning over him. She watched as his head banged repeatedly on the kitchen floor and urine spilled out of him. When Mouse regained consciousness, Misha licked him and rested her nose against his belly.

Mouse's health began to slip again. He went back to sleeping most of the day. He wasn't in pain, but his seizures left him weak and delicate. Misha had always spent a lot of her time in the house, but now she hardly ever left. And when she did go out, the first thing she did when she came back in was to find Mouse and position herself next to him.

It became increasingly difficult for me to leave for work. Mouse needed to have someone with him when he had a seizure. Over the years, Misha had adjusted to my leaving in the afternoons for the hospital. But after Mouse's surgery, she unadjusted and rebelled. She resumed her old tricks of trying to keep me at home, except she was even worse. Besides blocking the door and standing in front of my car, she started dirtying my white uniforms, yanking my pantyhose off my legs, and chewing on my stethoscope and nursing shoes.

It became so difficult for me to leave the house that I eventually gave up. After sixteen years of full-time and part-time nursing, I went on-call. Going on-call meant I only worked when I wanted to work. I gave up my scheduled hours, as well as my health insurance, pension plan, and vacation pay. Because Mouse was so sick and Misha was so anxious about my leaving the house, I didn't feel I had much of a choice. Drastically cutting back my hours at the hospital seemed like the next logical career move for me to make.

The doctors and nurses chided me for giving up a lucrative career so I could stay at home with my animals. Everyone said I was making a mistake. At my going-away party, my head nurse posted a big banner across the room that read, "You'll Be Back." When I clocked out on my last scheduled day, I wondered if maybe I was crazy, quitting my job for an epileptic cat.

After spending so many years of my life in a stressful, challenging profession, I suddenly found myself at home almost all the time. No CPR, no lifesaving IVs, no uniforms to get white, and no suppers to cook ahead for Mark. Now it was just a horse, a cat, and me. I was taking the road less traveled; I was starting my new, second life.

Misha helped me to care for Mouse. She supervised his feedings and helped me clean him up when he seized. She stood over him while he slept and nudged me when he woke up. And she tried to keep me from going anywhere, unless she came along. The first year I cut back to on-call, I rarely left the house, because whenever I did, Mouse would have a series of terrible seizures. My presence seemed to calm Mouse's nervous system and ease his epilepsy. Mark did a lot of the grocery shopping for me and he picked up library books that I ordered over the phone. I only worked seven ICU shifts that entire year.

The odd part was that I didn't miss going out. I couldn't imagine how I'd ever found the time to keep the house clean, the laundry washed, the fresh bread baked when I was working 32 hours a week. Now that I was staying home with Misha and Mouse, there were never enough hours in the day to get everything done. How had I ever managed to run a house when I was working? I adapted easily to hermithood; many weeks would go by without my talking to anyone face-to-face except Mark.

Mouse stabilized but continued to require a lot of attention. In between his care and my housework, I taught Misha some new tricks and taught myself how to play the classical guitar. Mark enjoyed having me at home when he got in from work at 5 P.M. He claims he gained twelve pounds from eating fancy suppers seven times a week.

Winter was brutal when it arrived. I refilled birdfeeders and deerfeeders three times a day and rode Misha out every morning to scatter ten pounds of corn for the wild turkeys and crows. House finches began dying from an avian disease that had reached epidemic proportions in Ohio. I'd trudge through the snow to find small, frozen finch carcasses upside down in a drift or stumble upon one that was weak, almost lifeless but still breathing. I'd bring the bird inside and force-feed it for two or three days. By then it was too late and it always died. Misha sniffed the dead and dying birds, unable to comprehend what was happening to them.

Then one frigid January morning, a chickadee flew hard into our living-room window. She fell in the snow and flailed about. I scooped her up and brought her into the warm house. Within an hour, she was fully recovered except she could not fly. Her right wing was dragging along beside her. I named the chickadee Dee Dee Myers (after President Clinton's press secretary) and stuck her on the branch of my lucky lemon tree, which I keep as a houseplant. When I was eleven years old, my grandfather stuck a lemon seed into a pot and after the seed sprouted, he gave it to me and said, "I want you to keep this plant so you will always remember me. When you are a grown-up lady and I am dead and gone, I want you to look at your lemon tree and say to yourself, 'My grandad gave me this. We loved each other very much.' "

My lucky lemon tree sat under a sky window. Next to the tree, on the floor, Mouse slept on Misha's blanket. Dee Dee Myers' favorite perch was directly above Mouse's head. Misha decided to stand guard beside them both. Mark began complaining because Misha was always in the living room. He told me he couldn't remember ever giving her his permission to wander through the rest of the house.

130

"She thinks her job is to watch over her Mouse. And since I can't have Mouse always under our feet in the kitchen, it's easier for him to stay by the lemon tree and let Misha go over there with him. She stands still and quiet. Misha won't hurt the living-room floor."

"Ha!" Mark guffawed. "I've heard that one before. Remember the kitchen floor? What about when she starts stomping ticks off her legs or she decides she wants to lie down on the braided rug? I refuse to crawl under this house to shore up this floor again."

"But Honey, what choice do I have? Mouse is dying and Misha wants to protect him. I promise I'll try to keep Misha from ruining the floor."

Mark curled up his lower lip and glowered. "You know there's nothing you can do to stop her when she has an itchy leg. Listen up. If you don't make her stay in the kitchen, she's going to break this floor. And when she does, I absolutely, positively will not fix it. You'll have to call a professional carpenter."

I didn't have the heart to move Misha away from Mouse, so I ignored Mark's proclamation. When two creatures find comfort in each other, it's not my place to interfere and break up their relationship. So I let Misha spend most of her day in the living room with the lemon tree looming over her head.

Meanwhile, I took Dee Dee Myers to the vet and asked him to x-ray her wing and set it in a cast. He laughed at me. "How in the world would you ever expect me to make a wild bird lie still long enough to be able to get an accurate x-ray?"

"Well surely it must be done all the time. What do people with rare and fancy parrots and macaws do when their birds break a wing?" I asked.

"They take them to expensive veterinary schools loaded with state-of-the-art equipment run by dozens of eager young students, where they receive a bill for thousands of dollars for elaborate medical services."

I was stunned. "You mean, local country vets like you can't set casts onto bird wings?"

"Nope."

"Well, I sure don't have a thousand extra dollars to spend at a vet school. What do you recommend?"

"What I usually do is fold the broken wing against the bird's body and tape it down for two weeks. Sometimes taping it will repair the break," he said.

"And sometimes it doesn't?"

He nodded.

"What if it doesn't work?" I asked.

"Then the bird lives the rest of its life with a broken wing."

"Do what you can," I said.

The vet folded Dee Dee Myers' wing and taped it against her side. He gave me a bottle of bird vitamins and a high-calorie seed.

"What do I owe you?"

"No charge," he said.

When Dee Dee and I got back home, Mark was in a dither. I asked him why. He said Mouse had two bad seizures and it upset Misha so much she ran around the house in a panic. "She broke the main floor beam and now our living room is collapsing."

"Oh honey, I'm sorry. I guess I shouldn't have left you alone with them." Mark barely heard me because by then he was grabbing tools, steel I-beams and extra car jacks. Minutes later, he disappeared under the house.

Everybody eventually settled down as our domestic drama came to an end. Mouse recovered from his two seizures, Misha was calmed, and Dee Dee Myers quickly learned to hop from branch to branch without using either of her wings. Mark propped up the floor so the main beam didn't break in two and by bedtime, Tresl life was back to normal.

Three weeks later I pulled the tape off of Dee Dee. Her wing was still broken and she could not fly. But she was so happy to be rid of that tight tape encircling her little feathered body that she chirped and flitted and preened. It looked like she'd be living with us permanently, so I got busy setting up proper chickadee accommodations.

I cut a wheelbarrow's worth of wild grapevines out of the woods and wound them into a tight circle. I pushed the circle of vines up into the lemon tree's sky window. I clipped fresh maple and beech branches and positioned them all around the big living-room window; then I connected the branches to the sky window with more grapevines via the lemon tree. This enabled Dee Dee to hop from window to window using a trail of grapevines so she'd never need to overtax her broken wing.

I put her sunflower seeds in a little wicker basket and hung it from a lemon tree branch; I laid a shallow dish full of water on the floor and left a grapevine tip touching the water bowl so Dee Dee could slide down it when she wanted a drink. Throughout the day, she amused herself by hopping onto Mouse and tugging at the fluffy fleece lining underneath him on Misha's horse blanket. Mouse would lift his head, sniff her, and go right back to sleep.

I knew nothing about keeping a bird, wild or domestic. So I ordered a dozen books from the library. None of them were much help until I found *Sharing a Robin's Life*. The author, Linda Johns, was a virtual bird-care professor.

When I finished her book, I still had more questions, so I wrote to Linda through her book publisher. She sent me a long, detailed letter packed full of wild-bird-care answers. Every time I had another question, I asked Linda, and she always answered me back. It soon became obvious that Linda and I were more than pen pals; we were kindred soul sisters who saw the natural world through the same sets of eyes. As my grandfather would have said, Linda and I were "coming from the same hymn book."

Linda told me Dee Dee had to have live bugs to eat. Mark stopped at the bait shop every week to buy her 100 maggots. I dug around the yard and in the eaves, scavenging spiders, caterpillars, and centipedes for her. Dee Dee learned to hop off her branch onto my hand and pluck out the wiggling bug I was holding for her. I loved the feel of her tiny scratchy toes wrapped tightly around my finger.

As we headed deeper into winter, the insects disappeared, and the bait shop closed for the season. I chased around in a panic, searching for maggot replacements, until I found the crème de la crème of bugs, wax worms. Mighty expensive—100 cost ten dollars—but Dee Dee loved them and she was worth every penny. She spent all winter hopping and rehopping on my hand, trying to mooch more wax worms out of my secret stash. Three times a month, our UPS man traveled our two miles of icy dirt road to deliver one itty-bitty box labeled *FRAGILE, LIVE.* He must have wondered what was in that box, but he never asked, and I didn't have the nerve to tell him.

It was lucky for me that I liked staying at home, because it was almost impossible for me to go out. Dee Dee's branches had to be refreshed and replaced every three days. Sometimes she'd fall off a branch, landing upside down on the floor and would have trouble getting right side up because of her floppy wing. I'd dash over to her when I heard her tumbling about and carry her back to her tree.

Mouse would occasionally get up out of Misha's blanket by way of Dee Dee's water bowl. He'd tip the bowl over, drench his back end and feet, and Dee Dee would have no water to drink. And if I wasn't watching her carefully, Misha would poke her head around in Dee Dee's branches, rip one out, and eat it. Or, if she was feeling furtive, she'd sneak her tongue into the sunflower-seed basket and gobble up Dee Dee's seeds when I wasn't looking.

When friends visited us, they were always shocked to see a 1,300-pound horse standing beside a 5-ounce bird and over an 8-pound cat in a corner of our living room. If anyone tried to approach my odd trio, Misha's ears would flatten and she would start to charge. She was protecting her bird and her cat, and no one except me was allowed near them.

Bored and full of energy, Dee Dee began leaping off her branches onto Misha's head and back. The first time she tried it, Misha shook her off. But Dee Dee was not to be dissuaded. She climbed up the grapevines until she was even with Misha's head, squatted and tucked up her broken wing, and then, with all her might, flung herself over onto Misha's mane. Misha stayed statue-still. Even when Dee Dee poked her bird toenails onto Misha's ears, Misha didn't budge. Soon Dee Dee was spending as much time perched on Misha's head as she did on her lemon tree branches.

When spring came, Dee Dee yanked out Misha's mane and tail hairs. It looked painful, but Misha never complained. Dee Dee would race up and down Misha's neck, pick out a perfect hair, snatch it, and race it over to her lemon tree. It looked as if Dee Dee were trying to build a horsehair nest, but without a mate, she never completed it.

I was busier than I had ever been, but my time was well spent. Mouse had stabilized, Dee Dee was thriving, and Misha was enjoying being a bodyguard for the two little animals. Every night I'd crawl exhausted into bed and wonder how I ever found the time to care for my animals when I worked. Giving up my part-time work at the hospital had been the right thing to do.

Chapter Fourteen

Six months passed before my head nurse and other ICU staffers were convinced that I would probably never come back to work full-time. And so friends from the hospital I hadn't seen in a while started visiting me. A lot of them wanted to see Misha-the-house-horse up close and personal. Many had already met Misha in the hospital parking lot, but few had made the twenty-mile trek out to our farm. The first spring after my "retirement," I was suddenly deluged with houseguests.

Hearing tales about a toilet-trained horse is one thing; seeing her in action is another. My visitors were overwhelmed by her size and impressed with her manners.

"She's huge," my charge nurse said.

"How do you keep the house so clean with this horse standing in the middle of it?" a cardiac rehab nurse asked.

"Does she bite?" an X-ray technician inquired sheepishly.

Seeing is believing, and when my co-workers left my house and went back to the hospital, they regaled all the other nurses and doctors with Jackie Tresl house-horse tales. I became a legend in my ICU. Now when I worked my one shift every two months, staff treated me like I was a small-town celebrity. Normally gruff and dismissive doctors stopped in mid-bustle to inquire about Misha. A thoracic surgeon in a rush to get home detoured into my patient's room to find out if Misha could count. And a radiologist I'd never even seen before interrupted his rounds to invite Misha and me out to the summer polo matches he held at his farm.

I said, "Misha doesn't play polo."

"She doesn't have to play. Just bring her out to enjoy the festivities. There will be sixty or seventy other horses for Misha to see. You and your husband will meet lots of great horse people, all of which are already fascinated by your housebroken horse," the radiologist said.

"How do your polo friends know about Misha?"

"I told them," Dr. Shelton said.

"But what did you tell them? You've never met Misha, have you? And you and I have never worked together, have we?" I asked.

"Ah, ah, ah . . . no, but so many of the ICU nurses talk about Misha that I feel like I know her. I just had to brag a little bit about her to the fellows I play polo with."

When I got off of work, I told Mark about the radiologist's invitation. He said, "I thought you didn't want to leave Mouse and Dee Dee home alone."

"Well, I don't. But I think it'll be a fun adventure. Besides, it seemed so important to Dr. Shelton that we come. He's told everyone about us."

"What did he have to tell? He's never even met Misha," Mark said.

"He shared some of the stories he's heard circulating through the hospital. He wants to show Misha off to his polo cronies."

Mark agreed to take us and asked me when I wanted to go. I was hoping for a cool, cloudy day so Misha wouldn't get overheated or be attacked by biting flies. I could only leave Mouse when he was out of his seizure cycle and neurologically stable. Dee Dee would have to be without wax worms for an entire afternoon because even

137

if I left her a bowl full of worms, she'd gobble them all down in the first ten minutes. Trying to coordinate my animals around a Sunday of polo was tough.

I watched the weather forecast every Friday until the kind of Sunday weather I wanted was predicted. Then I adjusted Mouse's anti-seizure medication so it would kick in right when we left the house. And I fed Dee Dee extra wax worms for breakfast so she wouldn't feel so deprived in the afternoon. As soon as Mouse was feeling sleepy and Dee Dee's tummy was full, we loaded Misha into her truck.

Misha hadn't been in the truck in almost a year and we had to drive an hour to get to Dr. Shelton's farm. Misha's legs were looking a bit unsteady when we finally arrived, but as soon as she saw all the polo horses, she whinnied with excitement. She had never seen that many horses gathered together in one spot. Misha was so eager to get out of the truck that she turned herself around and faced the back door even before the truck was parked.

Dr. Shelton's enormous house was perched on a hill overlooking thirty corrals and four polo fields. Cars, trucks, campers, and trailers were parked on every available inch of asphalt. There were polo ponies in the fields, the paddocks, and Dr. Shelton's back yard, ponies tied to hitching posts, sides of campers, trailer tongues, and board fences. Two dozen ponies were saddled up, ready to play polo while several dozen more were half "dressed," waiting in the wings for their turn. A hundred saddles were tossed around as five hundred people stood and sat amidst buzzing, hungry flies that swarmed in their faces.

Misha had just stepped out of the truck when I heard a voice boom out over a microphone. "Ladies and gentlemen, I present to you the first and perhaps only housebroken horse in all of America, standing 16 hands tall, a registered quarter horse, please welcome Misha, the mare that lives in the house."

All heads turned in our direction. People "ooohed" and "ahhhed." Kids rushed over. Unprepared for such an enthusiastic welcome, Mark and I were speechless, immobile, uncertain what to do next. Dr. Shelton snaked his way through the crowd and shook Mark's hand. He said, "I'm so glad you could make it. I've been telling my polo buddies all about you."

He swung his arm across Mark's shoulder and guided him over to meet the players. The last thing I heard as they were walking away was Dr. Shelton asking Mark if he'd like to join them in a game. I saw Mark shaking his head before he was swallowed up by silk sashes, mallets, and whips.

Misha and I visited with the children for a while, then meandered off on our own to explore the pony-filled paddocks. It was like walking through a mile-long mall or a state fairground or an airport runway that was packed tight with horses. There were so many of them it was surreal, and Misha was overwhelmed.

She and I wanted some time alone, so we found an isolated stream and stopped for a rest. An announcer's voice was calling the polo match and I wondered if Dr. Shelton had given Mark a helmet and stuck him on a pony. Misha looked sleepy so I stretched out on my back and we both took a short nap. Half an hour later, feeling rejuvenated and strong, we rejoined the polo merriment.

For the next two hours, someone was always strolling over to meet Misha. First they would introduce themselves to me, then immediately lose interest in me and latch onto Misha. She blossomed with all the attention and loved watching polo ponies being walked back and forth around her. Mark was perched on the bleachers, surrounded by a bunch of sweaty, muscled men, looking like he was having a good time. While people fawned over Misha, I watched polo.

It was odd to see such small horses carrying such large, athletic men. Before I went to Dr. Shelton's, all the male equestrians I knew liked their horses big and burly, geldings or studs, at least seventeen hands tall or better, which they rode wearing cowboy hats and western saddles. But the men here were different. Polo looked like a rough and rugged sport, but also seemed kind of strange. The ponies were short and their riders had to tilt sideways in the saddles to smack the baby-sized polo balls. Every once in a while, the match would stop abruptly and all the spectators would dash out onto the polo field to smooth over the holes in the grass made by the horses' hooves.

The spectators wore big, broad, beribboned hats, like the ones in My Fair Lady. The riders wore knee-high black leather boots and jodhpurs. Instead of drinking beer and pop, they sipped wine and champagne from real glass goblets and ate fancy cheeses, croissants, and caviar. Misha and I had suddenly been dropped into the middle of high society. And despite their wealth and prestige, these people wanted what I had; they longed for a house-horse of their own.

When the fourth match was over, Mark found us and grabbed my hand—his signal for "let's get out of here." We thanked Dr. Shelton, said our good-byes to the crowd and loaded Misha into her truck. Halfway home, Mark complained of a bellyache from all the Brie he had eaten.

"Brie? What's that?" I asked.

"Some kind of French cheese, I think. It was tasty, but now it's payback time for eating like a pig," he groaned.

When we came into the house, Mouse was waking up from his afternoon nap and Dee Dee was whistling for her wax worms. Misha was glad for the peace and quiet.

Our little house may have looked shabby compared to the pomp and opulence of polo, and there were no jodhpurs hanging in my closet or champagne chilling in my fridge, but Misha thought her home was grand.

Some of Dr. Shelton's friends called me after the polo match with questions on how to housebreak horses. After the first few calls, I started jotting down a few notes so I wouldn't forget any important training tips. But I shouldn't have bothered because it wasn't long before the polo people lost interest in house-horses and the telephone stopped ringing. Misha and I resumed our quiet, uninterrupted way of life while my list of training notes sat unused beside the phone.

In the afternoons, my "girls" liked to rest, which afforded me some time to myself. I spent those hours writing. Using my housebreaking tips as a template, I wrote a 1,000-word article. Then, I changed the angle and wrote a second article. Within a week, I had four Misha manuscripts, which I sent, along with pictures, to four different magazines. *Country* magazine bought one.

As soon as Misha's article appeared in *Country*, she began receiving fan mail from *Country* readers. Two people enclosed money and asked me to spend it on treats for Misha. Lots of readers sent me questions about housebreaking horses. I answered every letter and offered as many specific toilet-training details as I could.

My local librarian stopped me one day when I was browsing through the books. "Jackie," she said, "I read your *Country* article. I enjoyed it a great deal."

"Thank you," I said.

"Might we ask a favor of you?"

"Sure. I'll do anything I can to help the library."

"I was wondering if you would bring Misha inside the library for the Summer Reading Program and give a presentation about horses to ninety children between the ages of five and twelve."

"Ah, ah, ah . . . " I'd never done any public speaking and I didn't know how Misha would react to ninety energetic little kids. But I couldn't refuse the library after all the years of reading pleasure it had given me.

The librarian grinned when I accepted her invitation, then filled me in on the particulars of how long I was supposed to talk and on what topic. I promised to do my best.

She thanked me and said, "We'll expect to see you and Misha here in three weeks. Just wait until the Summer Reading Program hears about this. The children will be so excited."

I wrote out some horse-care notes on index cards, searched my bookshelves and gathered up all the animal books I'd read as a child. I decided my library presentation was going to focus on the power of books. If I hadn't read hundreds of books about animals and horses when I was a little girl, I might never have developed the imagination necessary to bring Misha inside the house.

I didn't know if the librarians would approve of my "books and horses" theme, but trusting my instincts, I took a chance. The kids sat slack-jawed with disappointment when Mark hauled in a big tarp and a stack of my old, tattered books. They were slightly more attentive when he laid the tarp across the library carpet. They sat up and gasped when Misha paraded through the entrance doors and they cheered and applauded when she positioned herself like a Michelangelo model on her tarp.

Misha had never spent an hour inside a federally operated building surrounded by crowds of people. I was hoping she wouldn't have an accident right on top of the library rug. The tarp was my "oops" precaution.

The children turned noisy and restless. Fifteen mothers were shouting to each other over the din. Several of them sported elaborate cameras and camcorders which were photographing and videotaping Misha and me while we stood there doing nothing.

Mark spent the whole hour hidden behind Misha's rump. He had agreed to come with me only as my back-up man. Crowds made him uncomfortable. My mouth was parched with fear, and terror weakened my knees. But this was Misha's day in the spotlight and she maximized her moment, standing proud and regal, exhilarated by her appreciative, adoring, pint-sized new fans.

142

The hour zipped by. The librarians beamed their approval when I held up my old books and talked about how important it is for children to read. I said that the books I read as a little girl taught me that animals are special. I explained that was why Misha got to live in the house because she, like all animals, deserves respect and kindness. I ended my presentation with Misha tricks, asking her to lift each foot on command, to turn in tight, graceful circles, to ring a bell, chew gum, and give me hugs and kisses.

The children were tickled. Their mothers came up to ask me a million questions about house-cleaning and horse-keeping. Not wanting to push my luck, I walked Misha outside to the back of the library, just in case she had to relieve herself, and invited the kids to pet her.

By the time we got home, Mark and I were as wrung out as dishrags. Misha was effervescent, peppy, and ready to spend the rest of her life being the center of attention. Mark and I dropped onto the couch. Misha stood over us and begged me to take her out for some more fun and glory. I made her a bowl of oatmeal and said, "I'm sorry Misha, this will have to do. We can't all be natural-born actresses like you."

She was disappointed and, after gobbling down her oatmeal, slunk outside to nibble dejectedly at the grass. For two weeks, Misha looked longingly and expectantly at her truck, hoping that sometime soon, she'd be back onstage at the Children's Summer Reading Program.

Chapter Fifteen

Mouse and Dee Dee Myers died within two weeks of each other. November was damp and gray and Mouse just couldn't seem to get warm even though I kept the heat set at eighty degrees. Misha and I sweated while Mouse's scrawny legs and ears felt icy cold. To keep him from shivering, I held Mouse in my lap for hours and hours, day after day.

Right before Christmas, his sniffles turned into a cold that deteriorated into pneumonia. It was his third bout with pneumonia in six months. I started him back on his ampicillin. He was already taking a daily steroid to strengthen his weak system, and phenobarbital twice a day to control his seizures.

Mouse hadn't had a good appetite for years. But when he contracted pneumonia, it was almost impossible for me to get any food down him. I spent all day and evening, off and on, trying to cajole him into swallowing half a teaspoon of baby food or a dribble of milk. Usually his refusal to eat was temporary. I was counting on the ampicillin to kill off his pneumonia bugs so he'd start taking a few bites of food for me. But this bout of pneumonia was different. The ampicillin didn't work and he couldn't seem to get well.

Mouse still staggered over to his litter box two or three times a day, and he loved to be cuddled in my lap. But mostly he just slept. Once a week, a violent grand mal seizure would wake him, but he was so debilitated, he didn't even seem to notice it. I knew my time with him was drawing to a close, but it was hard for me to let him go. He'd been with me eighteen and a half years, longer than I'd been a nurse and or had been married. Losing him would be hard.

Misha stopped hovering over Mouse. She stood far away from his blanket, giving him a lot of room, as if she had already said her good-byes to him. Some days Mouse would rally a little bit and I'd be encouraged, until Misha would nudge me, as if to say, "Mouse is dying. Don't get your hopes up."

Then, out of the blue, Dee Dee refused to eat her wax worms. She stopped climbing up into her sky window to hop around on her grapevines. She would perch on the same branch all day long and stare out the window, her focus riveted on some unknown spot. She might eat a few sunflower seeds and sip a thimbleful of water, but other than that, she was in a kind of hibernation.

When I added some avian antibiotics to her water, she wouldn't drink it. So I poured the medicine down the drain and let her be. She, too, was readying herself to die and there was nothing I could do to stop her. A few days later, her eyelids swelled shut and she could no longer see. That evening she fell out of the lemon tree and took her last gasping breath nestled in my hands. Sudden and swift, Dee Dee was gone.

My only comfort came in knowing I still had Mouse. With tears in my eyes from burying Dee Dee, I lay down on the floor beside Mouse and slept. I dreamed that Mouse was twenty-five years old, had a mouthful of teeth and could see and hear again. I woke up thinking all I had to do was find a cure for his pneumonia and Mouse would live for a couple more years.

The next ten days were horrible. Mouse wanted to die and I wouldn't let him. I started him on a second antibiotic and a different steroid. I forced watered-down baby food into his mouth with a syringe. When he developed diarrhea, I washed his bottom several times a day. And still, he got weaker and weaker.

Then one afternoon I sat him on the counter to give him his pill and when I pushed down on his body to steady his head, his back legs crumpled under him. He could no longer stand. Around midnight he started to cry, telling me he was in pain, begging me to end his misery.

I stayed up with him all night, trying to hold him in a more comfortable position so he wouldn't hurt. Misha stood beside us, nuzzling me while I sobbed. At sunrise, I called the vet and took Mouse in to him. The vet knew how much I loved Mouse and didn't have the heart to tell me it was time to put him to sleep. Instead he told me Mouse was dehydrated and gave me bags of IV fluids and tubing and showed me how to rehydrate him under his skin.

The last thing the vet said to me was, "Call me if there's anything else I can do. And whatever IV fluid you don't use, return it and I'll give you your money back."

What he was saying to me without putting it into words was that the end was near and all the IVs in the world wouldn't keep Mouse from death. My vet never suggested euthanasia; he knew I'd have to come to that decision on my own.

I kept Mouse in a box beside me for the next twelve hours. Every time I inserted the needle to administer IV fluids, he moaned. After three attempts, I stopped. He didn't want to be rehydrated. He wanted to die. His breathing was shallow and labored and he no longer opened his eyes.

With Misha at my shoulder, I injected Mouse with his two emergency syringes of Valium while he lay across my lap. His breathing slowed and he lost consciousness. Ten minutes later, he took one deep gasp for air. His heart stopped. My cat was dead.

I held him for a while longer until Mark gently took him from me. He went out and dug a grave. We wrapped him in an old winter jacket, and Mark laid Mouse to rest.

Then he came inside and held me while I cried harder than I had ever cried before in my life.

When I was growing up, my mother never allowed me to have pets, except once when she let me have a hamster. So Mouse had been the first furry love of my life. When I adopted him, I spent all my free time with him. I taught him to chase candies across the kitchen floor and bring them back to me. We played tag out through the kitchen door, across the front yard, and around again into the living room foyer. We cuddled in bed, on the chair, on the floor, and in the car. He helped me study for all my nursing exams, my chemistry tests, and my State Boards. He saw me in my wedding dress. I'd waited until my nineteenth birthday for a pet, and Mouse was my reward.

A naturally sunny person, I rarely get depressed or cry. So when I'm sad, Mark and Misha can't rest until I'm back to being my happy old self again. They don't know how to cope when I'm disconsolate. Misha tried all the tricks she usually uses to make me laugh, but none of them worked. Mark rented us some movies and bought me a special romaine salad at the grocery store. And for three minutes I'd be able to get Mouse out of my mind, but then I'd see my empty lap where my kitty used to love to lay and I'd start crying. Misha licked so many tears off my face that by the end of the day, I had red bumps all over my cheeks from where her rough tongue dragged itself a thousand times across my skin.

I knew I was overreacting and needed to get a grip on my emotions. After all, Mouse was old, and I'd had Dee Dee longer than I'd ever expected to. Still, I couldn't seem to get my mind off my loss. I knew I was in pretty bad shape when even reading books didn't help me forget.

By the third day, Mark was growing tired of my melodramatics. He wanted to get on with life and have me happy again. I tried to keep a smile on my face throughout breakfast, but cleaning up our granola bowls, I started to weep.

"Enough already," Mark hollered. "Look at how you've upset Misha. She feels so dejected by the way you're treating her, she isn't even mooching for her fair share of the granola."

I looked at her. Mark was right. Misha's head was drooping and her eyes looked dull.

She wasn't paying any attention to breakfast, normally one of her three most favorite meals. I went over and kissed her. She didn't kiss me back.

"But what can I do?" I asked Mark. "I don't want to be this sad, but I can't seem to stop thinking about Mouse."

"How about we go to the shelter and you pick yourself out another pet?"

"Really? You'd let me get another pet so soon after Mouse? You told me last month you didn't want any more animals for a while, that Misha was plenty enough for us."

"Well, I was wrong. You're miserable and Misha and I are suffering because of it. I think you need a new little fur ball to love."

"Oh, honey, thank you. You're the best. Yes, let's do it. Let's go to the shelter right now."

I had never been inside an animal shelter and assumed, as do many other animal-lovers, that they were horribly grim places filled with cats and dogs destined only to be put to sleep. But when it came time to adopt a new pet, getting it from the shelter seemed like the best and only place to go. Mark and I could make a difference in at least one unwanted animal's life; we could spare one poor soul from euthanasia.

We walked in and saw forty pens loaded with dogs and puppies of every pure and mixed breed known to man. There were registered rottweilers, poodles, cocker spaniels, and a greyhound nursing eight puppies. Dogs were barking, jumping, and sleeping, but as soon as we approached their cages, they stepped up to nuzzle our fingers, begging us to choose them.

Behind the dog kennel was a large room lined floor to ceiling with cages. Every cage contained an adult cat or a couple of tiny kittens. All feline eyes peered directly into ours. Every cat we took out of its cage purred and cuddled in our arms.

Half an hour later I asked Mark if we could take a break and walk outside for some fresh air. The shelter was emotionally taxing. How would I ever be able to pick just one of these animals, especially knowing that almost all the others would probably die? Every cat and dog in the shelter longed for a loving home and yearned to live. It made me cry.

Mark said, "Stop bawling. Quit focusing on the animals that you can't take home. Instead, concentrate on picking out the one you really want. Just think, you have an opportunity to save any animal in there and make it part of our family."

I sniffled. "But it's so hard to choose."

"I realize that. But that's why we're here. Now let's focus on finding you a new pet," Mark said.

"But I don't even know if I want a cat or a dog, a puppy or a kitten."

"Keep an open mind and pick out whichever one you love the most."

Mark may not belong to MENSA, but in my book, he's brilliant. There I was, standing in the shelter parking lot acting like a blubbering idiot until Mark directed my energies and refocused me. The logic of what he said made perfect sense and I was ready to adopt.

I don't know how much time most people spend inside the shelter searching for their new pet, but I'm guessing I stayed longer than the average. Four hours later, after holding and petting at least forty different animals, I had narrowed down my choice to three cats, a dog, and three puppies. The fifth hour was the most grueling because now I had to pick just one. I asked Mark to help me choose.

"I must say, I'm partial to that little brown puppy."

"Really? That's kind of my favorite, too," I said.

Over by itself, away from most of the other cages, sat a five-
pound, shy and shivering pup. The sign on its cage said it was a
female Labrador mix. I asked the shelter worker how big she would
get. "About seventy-five pounds."

Mark and I frowned. "That's an awful big dog for us. We were
hoping for something smaller."

But we pulled the little gal out anyway and held her again. She
was timid and hid her nose into my neck and then into Mark's. Her
tummy felt round and her feet smelled delicious. She stared in our
eyes when we talked to her.

I said, "Well, she'll be bigger than we wanted, but I think she's
the one for me."

Mark nodded. "I agree. She's a keeper."

The shelter worker was pleased. She said, "This little pooch had
one more day before her number was up. I would have hated to put
her to sleep because she's one of my favorites. We're always so happy
when we can send our animals to a good home with people who will
love them."

The shelter wouldn't let us have her right away. First they had
to give her a flea bath, a vaccination, and worm her. "Come back in
an hour or two so she'll have plenty of time to dry off before you take
her out in this cold weather."

We hated to leave our pup, even for five minutes. But since we
didn't have any dog food in the house, we used the time to go buy
some. Mark and I were giddy with excitement. We'd be bringing
home our first dog ever, and a baby at that.

Pet stores cater to people like us. Everything we saw we wanted,
especially the latex toys and doggie treats. We picked out a tiny red
collar, a bag of puppy food, a plastic carrot squeak toy, and a sack of

thin rawhide for her teeth. Thirty minutes later, we were back at the shelter.

"Can we have our puppy now?" I asked.

"But she's not dry," the worker said.

"Don't worry. We'll make sure she stays warm."

We were so excited that the shelter staff didn't have the heart to make us come back an hour later. They handed our pup over to Mark, who slipped her down the front of his winter jacket and zipped it closed.

The shelter workers laughed. "Isn't she gonna get you all wet? Then you'll be cold."

Mark said, "I don't mind. My wife needs a new pet to love and I want to get both of them home."

We were like newlyweds driving back, giggling and cuddling in the car as we fussed and poked at the pup. Like magic, my tears were gone and a big smile filled my face. I hadn't thought about Mouse for six whole hours. Later, when I did think about him, I thought how his dying had saved the life of our new pup. His death had given her life.

Chapter Sixteen

For two days, Misha had been an "only child." Even though I'd spent much of that time crying, she enjoyed having my undivided animal attention for the first time ever. I knew that if we didn't hurry and adopt another pet, Misha would soon become a spoiled brat. Nature abhors a vacuum, and Misha was quickly learning how to fill the void left from Mouse's death by demanding all my time and energy.

I wondered how she'd react to a puppy. Misha had trotted around neighborhood dogs all her life, but she'd never had to share her house with one. And since baby animals tend to get all of their owners' attention and love, I was worried that Misha might feel left out and jealous. On our way home from the shelter, Mark and I promised each other that

we'd be sensitive to Misha's feelings. Our plan was to involve Misha as much as possible with our new dog so she wouldn't feel discarded. I would continue to take her out, just the two of us together, grazing and riding, leaving the pup at home. I wanted Misha to know that she was number one and the new puppy a distant second. As my grandfather used to say:

"Make new friends, but keep the old,
One is silver and the other gold."

Now that Mouse was dead, Misha was the "old" and had rightfully earned the status of gold. Even though the puppy was lovable and sweet, being the newcomer, she ranked as silver.

Misha knew something was up as soon as we stepped out of the car. She hustled over, sniffed me, kissed me, and left to examine Mark. Figuring he must be the source of the new and unusual smell, she stuck her nose down in his jacket, discovered a fur ball, and nudged it. The puppy whimpered and burrowed deeper into Mark to get away from the offensive bewhiskered horse nose. Misha heard the whimper and backed away, spooked and confused. I think she initially thought Mouse had returned from the dead and Mark was hiding him in his coat. But when the animal she nudged didn't meow, she was temporarily bewildered.

It didn't take long before she understood this was a newcomer about to invade her house and, since Mark was toting it around in his coat, the newcomer would probably stay a while.

Once we were all inside the house, the puppy did not want to be put on the floor, the chair, or the couch; she wanted to be held. Whenever Misha tried to sniff or touch her, the puppy cowered. I asked Mark to sit and cuddle the puppy in his lap so I could spend time reassuring Misha.

I hated having to ignore the puppy, but for the first few days, that's what I did. I'd sneak in a few snuggles or a game of plastic carrot when Misha was out grazing, but Misha was staying pretty much glued to my side and I had to relegate the majority of the puppy's care to Mark. It was vital that Misha never feel unloved.

Mark took some vacation time from work to nurture the pup. Everywhere he went—the hardware store, the grocery, or the library—he carried the puppy against his chest in two large bandannas he kept pinned around his neck. He cradled her in the crook of his arm when he was at home so I never had to worry that Misha might accidentally step on her.

We had trouble choosing a name for our puppy. At seven pounds, ten inches long, and still so young, it was hard to know what name would suit her personality when she grew up. Our puppy was faint-hearted and cried when no one was holding her. Every night she tunneled under the bedclothes and pressed herself up between us both while we slept. She was petrified of strangers, loud noises, sudden movements, and food bowls. She backed away whenever we set a dog dish down in front of her and would only eat when we fed her out of our hands. Mark didn't think it was prudent to always hand-feed her, so I started stashing small piles of food underneath chairs and in dark corners of the kitchen. The puppy loved to sniff out the tidbits and gobble them up. If I put the same tidbits into a bowl, she'd run away, as if she'd seen a python.

Mark said, "She acts like she's part rodent, sneaking off into dimly lit, cobwebby corners to eat." And so, in jest, he started calling her Our Little Rodent. A few days later, I too was referring to her as Our Little Rodent. It soon became her unofficial, temporary name.

We planned on picking out a different name for her, but before we knew it, she got used to coming to us when we called her Rodent. The name kind of stuck. We had hoped for something more feminine or poetic, but since she seemed happy with it, we never changed it.

Ten days after we brought her home from the shelter, Mark went back to work and I was left alone with Misha and Rodent. I figured we'd bond best if we went out grazing together. So for a few hours every day, I'd stick Rodent into my down vest, sit in a snow-covered pasture, and watch Misha while she ate.

The first few times, I brought a book. But Rodent wanted me to scratch her ears and kiss her delectable nose, and I never had any free time to read. Rodent loved to climb over my body like I was her small mountain, pausing now and then to chew on my bootlaces, my hat, and my mittens. Misha kept her eye on me, saw me playing with and petting the puppy, but was so grateful for our company that she never seemed to mind.

After a few days, Rodent started wandering away from me to get closer to Misha. It was hard to sit by and watch a tiny puppy lie inches away from Misha's hooves. I figured Rodent would have to learn for herself how to be safe around an animal that was one thousand times her size, so I bit my nails, pulled out my hair and let the two animals interact.

It wasn't long before Rodent wanted to be with Misha just as much as she wanted to be with me. Soon I was sitting almost pressed against Misha's legs so Rodent could lie between us. By the end of the week, Rodent was biting off blades of grass and eating it. The puppy and the horse grazed together. Misha was protective of Rodent and never came close to stepping on her.

Once Mark went back to work, I couldn't ride Misha because I didn't want to leave Rodent alone. Misha soon became restless from a lack of exercise, so I decided to try to take Rodent riding with me. She was so small that I was able to stretch out my elastic waistband, stick the lower two-thirds of her body down the front of my sweatpants, and push her shoulders and neck up through the bottom of my coat. I had to shift my weight and use more of my back muscles riding this way, but after a few miles I got used to my center of gravity being shifted.

When I first rode with Rodent, I kept Misha at a slow trot, afraid I'd be unbalanced with Rodent's by-then twelve extra pounds around my middle. But my thigh muscles soon strengthened, holding tight around Misha's ribs, and eventually Rodent and I built up to going five miles at a canter.

We became inseparable. Rodent assumed she was part horse because she spent so much time with Misha. I'd toss out a pile of hay and Rodent would sprawl across the middle of it, forcing Misha to eat around the edges. Sometimes when Misha wanted to reach a particularly succulent flake of clover, she would try to nudge Rodent off, but Rodent never moved far away. Misha was often forced to pull the hay she wanted out from under the puppy's body.

When Misha ate her breakfast pancakes or doughnuts, she usually took such big bites that pieces of food would drop out of her mouth. Rodent learned to wait underneath Misha's head to pick up all the crumbs Misha dropped. Rodent wouldn't eat Misha's treats if I offered them to her, but let food fall from Misha's mouth and Rodent gobbled it up.

Babies do grow up, and soon Rodent wouldn't fit inside the waistband of my sweatpants any more. The day came when I broke my vest zipper trying to zip it around her. That was the last time she rode in my clothes. I tried again to leave Rodent home with Mark when I went riding, but as soon as I left, Rodent cried as if her heart were breaking. The second day I rode without her, Mark turned his back for twenty seconds and our seventeen-pound puppy was gone. He jumped into the car and found her two and a half miles from home, her nose to the ground, tracking Misha's scent along the dirt road I had just ridden over.

Mark was still angry at Rodent when Misha and I returned home. "I'm going to tie that dog up the next time you leave her here with me. She could have been run over by a car or lost forever trying to follow you and Misha. It's just pure luck I managed to find her."

I didn't want the puppy tied up. That would only traumatize her more. And Mark had so many farm chores he needed to do, I couldn't ask him to sit and cuddle Rodent every time I went riding. So I bought some corduroy material and sewed it into a pooch pouch. I made a drawstring top and stitched two wide straps onto it. I slid all of Rodent's body except her head into the pouch, slipped the straps over my shoulders, and flopped the sack and pup against my chest. I couldn't wear the pouch as a backpack because having an extra twenty pounds behind me made me dangerously unbalanced when I rode. The one time I tried to carry Rodent on my back, Misha turned abruptly and the puppy, the pouch, and I were flung off. For some reason known only to gravitational physicists, having Rodent's weight hanging down my front instead of my back allowed me to maintain my balance.

For the next couple of months, I rode Misha while carrying Rodent in her pouch. Since she gained weight gradually, my shoulder and thigh muscles had time to adapt. I got so strong I could stay atop Misha with Rodent even when Misha galloped. Lugging a small dog around the front of my chest made me a more powerful rider.

When Rodent weighed twenty-seven pounds, my shoulders and neck started aching after short rides. When she reached thirty pounds, my chest muscles protested and would no longer support her. I tried once more to leave her with Mark. He didn't pay any attention to her and when I came home, she was near hysteria.

"Do you think you could make time to sit and play with Rodent when I go riding?" I asked Mark.

"Would that be before I bring in a load of firewood or after I change the master cylinder on the truck?"

"Don't you ever have any free time?"

"Honey, I'm sorry. I have so much to do; I'm behind on everything that needs doing. Just tie her up when you go. She'll be fine," Mark said.

I couldn't. Rodent was so attached to Misha and me that it would be emotionally cruel for us to abandon her. So I told Rodent she could come along, but she'd have to learn to ride.

We started out at a walk. I stood Rodent in front of me with her torso straddling Misha's withers. I kept my arms up like porch railings so she wouldn't fall off, but I didn't hold her. She had to learn to balance herself and not rely on me. If Misha were to leap or balk, Rodent had to be responsible for maintaining her own, independent seat.

Initially, Misha fussed and complained about Rodent's puppy toenails. When Rodent dug them in to get a good grip, Misha refused to walk forward. But after several grueling sessions, it seemed to dawn on Misha that she didn't have a choice; the puppy and I were going to ride her whether she liked it or not. Misha finally did accept Rodent's nails in her back, but she needed one favor in return. She wanted Rodent to face left. For some reason, Rodent's front feet positioned on the right side of Misha's withers hurt a lot more than when the puppy kept her front feet left of the withers. I made Rodent always point herself to the left and after that, Misha carried her without complaint.

Summer arrived and Rodent stopped growing. When I asked my vet, he said Rodent would never weigh more than forty pounds. I was glad the animal shelter's estimate of seventy-five pounds was wrong because the bigger she got, the harder it would be for her to stay perched on Misha's back.

Bug season came. Misha preferred to canter when the flies were bad so that she'd be going too fast for them to bite her. Rodent was still learning to ride, and I wanted Misha to walk. She bickered whenever I tried to slow her down, so I finally gave up and let her run. I briefly kept one arm wrapped around the pup to steady her, but then I stopped, forcing Rodent to use her own muscle power to stay on Misha's back. It wasn't long before we were cantering twelve miles over dusty dirt roads every few days.

Misha wasn't able to run as fast or as fluidly when Rodent was on her back. She powered herself less from the rear and more with her front legs. The adjustment in her stride helped the puppy ride steady and safe. Misha always preferred that I ride her alone, but she cooperated in making Rodent feel welcome. Perhaps Misha knew how much Rodent worshipped her.

Early on Misha had to learn how not to step on an active, bouncing puppy inside the house. One minute Rodent would be chewing a rawhide under the counter; five seconds later she'd be flopped under Misha's hooves. Even I had trouble keeping track of her. One evening I was getting Misha ready for bed. I had unrolled her three rugs on the porch when Rodent came scurrying in. Misha had just turned to face her double-swinging door when she accidentally stepped on Rodent's tiny front paw. Misha never even saw the puppy coming.

Rodent shrieked, which frightened Misha. She froze in place still standing on the puppy's paw. It took me half a minute to yank Misha's hoof away so Mark could swoop down to gather Rodent in his arms. He laid her on the bed so I could examine her for broken bones. Misha looked forlorn and came over to be with us. The puppy whimpered. Her paw wasn't broken, but the soft tissue around the joint was swelling up. I gave her an eighth of an aspirin. We lay across the bed cuddling the pup and, so Misha wouldn't feel left out, I let her stand beside the bed with us.

The next morning when Mark left for work, Rodent's foot was puffy and she didn't want to walk on it. I was feeling lazy and decided the puppy and I would lounge around in bed all morning. I couldn't have Misha standing in the living room all by herself, so I invited her over to the bed. Around noon I got up, did my housework, and crawled back into bed. When Mark got home from work, Misha's nose was resting beside me on his pillow.

"Are you sick?" he asked.

"No."

"Then why are you still in bed?"

"The girls and I were feeling sluggish and the puppy's paw is swollen."

"Why is Misha standing beside the bed? She already has the run of the rest of the house. Now she needs to be in here, too?"

"I couldn't very well ostracize her. You agreed we'd treat her like she's golden and keep her involved in raising Rodent," I said.

"Yes, that's all well and good. But the bedroom floor can't take her weight. How many times do I have to tell you this house was not engineered to hold a 1,320-pound horse?"

When Mark scolded me, Rodent whimpered and Misha laid her ears back. I said, "You don't have to be so mean. I didn't let Misha stomp or wander around unattended. She's been standing ladylike and quiet the whole day."

Mark sighed and went to take a bath. I carried the puppy into the kitchen and started dinner. Misha followed behind to help me roll out pizza dough. She loves to lick up the flour that's left over from kneading. Her tongue and lips were covered with white powder when Mark sat down at the table.

I apologized and kissed him before plopping the puppy with her swollen paw into his lap. Misha left the counter to join in on the merrymaking. She gave Mark a juicy, sticky, glutinous flour kiss while Rodent licked Misha's cheek and Mark's chin.

"Aren't we the luckiest people in the world? How does it feel to be part of a kissing fest and have so many females loving you?" I asked.

"Yeah, right, you put them up to this so I'll forget to be mad. But I won't forget when the bedroom floor collapses." He smiled and kissed Misha back.

I lapsed into a bad habit of reading books and cuddling the puppy in bed all morning while Misha dozed beside us. Some days I felt guilty that Mark was slaving away at work while I was lounging, but I rationalized my behavior by telling myself that Rodent and I were bonding. Misha loved our "bed" time, too. As soon as I'd wiggle back under the covers, she'd march over from the kitchen and lay her nose onto our pillows. If I stayed in bed for six hours, she stood beside the bed for six hours.

The year before, Mark bought us an outside wood burner that

pumped 190-degree water through underground pipes into baseboards that lined the walls of our house. I loved the luxury of turning the thermostat up to eighty degrees, closing the drapes, grabbing a book and the puppy, and going back to bed. It wasn't long before Misha started lying down too, not on the bed but on the braided rug in front of it.

Misha's body temperature is two degrees warmer than mine, and with her gut always busy digesting hay, she's like a portable heater. With the combination of my three layers of bedclothes, my flannel granny nightgown, the furry puppy pressed up against me, and Misha warming the air around me, the bedroom was like an oven. Each day I'd vow not to sleep longer than an hour, but the heat, dark, and quiet lulled the three of us into a deep, semi-hypnotic, all-morning sleep.

We always got up by early afternoon. I reorganized my farm chores, housework, and baking so that I could get them all done in less than three hours. By the time Mark walked through the door at suppertime, it looked like I'd been productive and busy all day long. I couldn't bring myself to confess I'd spent much of my morning in bed.

Misha got used to being in whatever part of the house I was. Since Rodent was allowed to follow me from room to room, I didn't have the heart to tell Misha she couldn't do the same. Before we adopted Rodent, I didn't let Misha wander through the house because she'd fiddle with my books, the TV, and anything else that she could fit between her lips. But when I was teaching Rodent not to chew on newspapers or pull on electrical cords, Misha must have been paying attention. By the time the puppy was nine months old, Misha could be left unsupervised beside my biggest bookcase or the bundle of stereo wires.

Misha started spending every evening in the living room with us. I waited for Mark to protest, but he didn't. While I held Rodent in my lap and read, Misha rested her chin on Mark's shoulder while he watched TV. None of us moved around much until our 9 P.M. snack time. Then Misha and Rodent came alive.

Most nights I served Mark a tray of fruit, dried noodles, and peanuts to snack on during the late local news. Misha liked to position herself three inches from Mark's chin, letting her saliva drip into his lap. Every few minutes, Mark would slip her a piece of apple or a peanut. With Rodent also mooching, snack time became complicated.

Misha loved Rodent as long as food wasn't involved. When it was time to beg for treats, Misha wanted Rodent out of her way. Misha never hurt her, but she'd nudge her and toss her to the other side of the room. It was uncharacteristic of Misha to be aggressive towards an animal. However, Rodent was the first animal we'd ever had that liked to eat the same foods that Misha did. Mouse had been strictly a meat and baby-food cat, and Misha couldn't stomach Dee Dee's maggots and wax worms. But when we adopted Rodent-the-omnivore, mealtimes and snack times became competitive.

Rodent developed wily ways to beg covertly. Sometimes she'd hide under Mark's chair and stick her nose up between the slats to mooch a bite. Other times she'd hang back, then make a mad dash between Misha's legs and lick Mark's fingers for a taste of whatever he was eating. Or she'd unexpectedly leap up into Mark's lap and hope he'd protect her from Misha's bossy nose. But as soon as Misha saw Rodent get a bite of anything, trouble ensued.

Misha would let Rodent eat a peanut if Mark gave Misha several of her own. Rodent was allowed a small pile of noodles as long as Misha got a bigger pile. And it was okay to peel and cut an apple slice into puppy-sized pieces for Rodent if Misha got one entire apple all to herself. If Misha thought Mark was dividing his snacks unequally, if it looked as though the puppy was getting part of what Misha thought she should have, Misha stomped around Mark's chair, lunging and bullying Rodent, trying to place herself between Mark and the dog.

One evening when Misha was rushing at a dropped peanut, trying to get to it before Rodent did, I heard the plywood around Mark's chair snap. Two evenings later, the floor under the TV cracked, and Mark watched *Jeopardy* lopsided. The floor soon sagged around the bed from Misha lying down and napping beside us.

It became difficult to vacuum the rugs because the floor was cupped down in so many spots. A lot of the dirt wouldn't suck up because the vacuum rolled over the high spots, leaving the low spots unclean. When I walked quickly through the house, the floor creaked and swayed under my feet.

Mark refused to comment on this latest bit of horse-related architectural destruction. He moved the TV over to a spot where the floor was still level, and he avoided walking where the plywood was bowed.

Finally, I asked, "We'll probably have to do something about the floor pretty soon, won't we?"

"We? What are you planning to do?"

"Well, nothing, but I'll help you, of course."

"And what do you suggest I do? Your horse has ruined this floor."

"Can't you prop it up with some more car jacks?" I asked.

Mark grimaced and sighed deeply. "First of all, I only had four extra, and they are all in use. Two are jacking up the kitchen and the other two are jacking up the floor around your grandfather's lemon tree. Do you want me to go out and buy more jacks? As bad as this floor is, we'll probably need ten more."

"Ten jacks? That sounds like an awful lot of money. Isn't there any other solution?" I asked.

"Yes, Missy, there is. We put in a whole new floor made with hardwood boards placed close together, with a steel I-beam running the length of the house."

"How do we do that? Do we live in one half of the house while you fix the other half?"

"No, we'd have to move out."

"Move out? But where would we go? There's no place we could go that Misha would be allowed to live with us, except maybe the rental house, but the tenants' lease isn't up for another seven months."

"Yes, there is another place. We can move into our barn," Mark said.

"But, but, but . . . it's a barn."

"I know it's a barn, but it has hot and cold running water. It's the perfect solution. We can all live together while I replace the joists and flooring."

I was speechless, dumbfounded, subsumed with dread.

"It's kind of your fault the floor is destroyed, and we don't have a lot of other options. If we don't get the floor fixed soon, you and Misha will be standing on the ground, cooking my dinner while old broken floor boards fall around your ankles."

Mark had decided it would be so. Our fate was sealed. For the next three months, a forty-year-old husband and wife, along with their horse and their dog, set up housekeeping in a barn.

Chapter Seventeen

I t took us four months to get moved out into the barn. Mark drew up plans and design specifications for the new house floor. He milled dead-standing oak and hickory trees from our woods into two-inch-wide boards and welded heavy-duty metal floor joist brackets out of angle iron. While the boards finished drying, he shopped for plywood, additional insulation, horse-tough linoleum, and mud-resistant carpeting. He modified the plumbing in his barn so he could hook my washing machine up to his shop sink. My job was to pack.

We hadn't moved in fourteen years and even though I'd never allowed clutter to accumulate, there was an awful lot of "stuff" to be put into boxes. We would store more than half of our belongings in our machine shed; the rest I'd need to turn the barn into our home. Determining what I'd need to accomplish that was tricky, especially when it came time to pack the books.

I tried to think ahead, imagining which books I'd need during our summer of reconstruction. All my life I've owned bushels of books and have taken it for granted that when I was in the mood to read a favorite poem or look at a map of Indonesia, I could just reach up and pull a book off my shelf. But now I had to pack most of my books away. I could only keep a short shelfful in the barn.

How could I ever know which ones to pick? Would there be

strange birds in July or unusual wildflowers in August that I'd want to identify? Would one dictionary with 155,000 entries be enough or would there be times when I'd need my fat unabridged Webster's with its 320,000 definitions and its full-color maps of the world? How many cookbooks and medical texts should I keep? Would I find myself suddenly desperate for a Shakespearean sonnet or a chapter from *Walden*? It reminded me of the oft-repeated question, "If you were stranded on a desert island and could only take three books with you, which books would you choose?" I spent a week sorting and re-sorting. In the end, I permitted myself sixteen books for my life in the barn.

Ready at last to move out of the house, we discussed whether Misha would sleep in the barn or on her porch at night. Because Mark built Misha's porch so strong to begin with, it didn't need any repair. There was no physical reason why Misha couldn't continue to sleep on it and logistically, it was the simplest solution for us. But Misha had other ideas and refused to be that far away from us at night.

My challenge was to find a way Misha could sleep in the barn and maintain her housebreaking. Misha rarely ever relieved herself in the barn, but whenever she did we didn't scold her because, after all, a barn is a barn. I had to teach her that the barn was now our house and she had to go outside to do her business. The only way she could get outside was if we left the barn doors open at night. And with the doors open, we wouldn't be able heat the barn. Letting Misha sleep in the barn with us meant we would be waking up to some very chilly mornings. But as Mark is fond of saying, "If it was easy to have a house-horse, everyone would have one."

Mark built both our house and barn out of fifty-foot-high poplar trees that he cut out of our woods. He milled the logs flat on two sides and chiseled notches in the ends before stacking them into walls. Unlike our house, the barn was two and a half stories tall, and had massive handmade elm doors. There was a work sink inside, but no bathtub or toilet. So when we moved out of our house, Mark "borrowed" our bathtub and set it sixty feet from the barn. He attached two garden hoses to the hot and cold water faucets in the barn sink and led the hoses out to the tub. The woods, a shovel, and a roll of toilet paper served as our summer bathroom.

Mark took the old living-room rug from inside the house and laid it on the concrete floor of the barn. I spread two other area rugs near the barn doors where Misha was going to sleep. In a flat area outside, in front of the barn doors, I asked Mark to string a single strand of high-tensile wire between the trees, attaching one end to the outside barn wall. At the other end of the wire, I had him hang a chain across the opening so that Misha could either be free to come and go, or be kept inside.

At night, Misha slept on three layers of rug, right inside the open barn doors. When she wanted to do her business, she only had to walk five feet to get outside. At night I kept the chain up so she wasn't wandering around in the fields, unsupervised. During the day I took the chain down so that whenever she wanted to, she could go out to graze or come back in the barn to snooze. I had to be vigilant in making sure she knew her bathroom was still outside.

I was concerned that living in the barn might be unsafe for Rodent. Even though she slept in bed with us, every once in a while, at sunrise, she'd feel hot and jump down onto the cool kitchen floor. What would happen if she did that while we were in the barn? Would she leave our bed and wander outside through Misha's open barn doors? The night woods are a dangerous place for a sheltered, timid dog. I'd never had to worry about her getting out when we lived in the house. There she would have had to push open Misha's double-swinging door, which was impossible for her to do because she wasn't strong enough.

It took us three days to get settled into the barn. I had to establish safe places, out of Misha's reach, to store groceries, medicine, cleaning supplies and dishes. I had to find an unsullied surface to knead bread and roll out piecrust and I had to allocate a dark corner for Rodent's food. It was my job to bring comfort, domesticity, and routine to a barn.

Mark thought it would take him one month to replace the floor. Instead, it took him three months because he decided that while we were all moved out, he'd install four skylights, add some insulation into the eaves, and replace a leaky section of the roof. Some mornings when I woke up my fingertips were numb, the thermometers inside and out reading forty-nine degrees. I'd put the teakettle on to boil and wrap myself into multiple layers of clothes. Mark would wake up laughing at me in my two pairs of sweat pants, flannel shirts, sweaters, and arctic socks, with a big woolly bathrobe corseted over top of it all.

Two weeks into the renovation, our town had its worst flood in history. We had no electricity for three days. Powerless, we relied on a battery-operated radio and only turned it on in the evenings to hear a weather update.

On one of those evenings, we heard a report that we'd hoped we would never hear. A tornado had just touched down two miles from our house and was heading in our direction. Rodent was already shivering, scared by the ear-splitting thunderbolts cracking all around the barn. Misha stayed huddled up close to us, her ears pointed towards the radio. We talked about running for cover in a cave that was nestled into the ravine beside our house, but Misha would never be able to fit into it. Since we wouldn't have been able to bring her with us, we decided to stay in the barn and take our chances, the four of us, together. Trapped, there was nothing we could do but wait.

The tornado never touched our farm. It veered south and missed us by an eighth of a mile. The heavy winds brought down a lot of our trees, and torrents of rainwater washed all of the gravel down and off our long driveway. Birds' nests littered the field; unhatched eggs were tossed into the grasses. I found a few unfeathered baby birds, but, cold and wet, they didn't survive for more than an hour.

Misha hates it when the electricity goes out. She likes to have plenty of light in the evening and enjoys a brisk fan blowing on her when the weather is hot and humid, as it was after the flood. She doesn't get any home-baked cookies or potato pancakes when the electric stove has no power to run. And she prefers to drink her water out of the bathtub while Mark and I are taking our baths. Without electricity, the pump can't raise water up from the well, we can't take baths, and Misha can't drink bath water.

Living way out in the country, our power goes off about eight times a year, usually for only a few hours. But every other year, it will be off for three days, leaving Misha miserable the whole time. Living in the barn without electricity turned her fussy and irritable. No more strawberry crepe breakfasts and homemade pizza suppers, she had to eat cold toaster pastries and jelly sandwiches. No more opera in the afternoon or newscasts in the evening.

Mark rigged a work light to a car battery so I could read after dark. Misha hung over me, sharing my wattage like a coal miner trapped in a mine without her own light. I had to conserve our water, and Misha had to drink hers out of a pail. Eventually she went on strike, and until the electricity went back on, she would only drink water out of puddles in the yard.

A week before the flood, I had picked, shelled, and frozen eighty pounds of peas from my garden. My freezer was packed. We had an ancient gas generator that worked sporadically and spastically, but Mark was forced to keep it running to save my peas. He spent hours repairing the generator, changing its spark plugs, cleaning its carburetor, and shifting leaky fuel lines. It limped along, and my peas never defrosted.

When the electricity did come back on, Misha almost cheered. I baked her some oatmeal cookies and left *National Public Radio* turned on all afternoon. She gave me a kiss of gratitude with raisins and rolled oats smeared between her horsey teeth.

Soon after we moved into the barn, my regional newspaper hired me to do some freelance writing for them. The editor started me on a ten-part series about the flood. It was a great opportunity and I jumped at the chance. The only potential drawback was Rodent. She would have to come with me as I followed leads and conducted interviews.

Rodent had never been left alone at home. One of us was always with her. Being abandoned as a baby and caged at the animal shelter for weeks, her separation anxiety was worse than Misha's. Since I enjoyed the luxury of not having to go to work, Mark and I decided the day we adopted her she would never be separated from us.

When it was time for me to write my newspaper series, Mark was busy working on the floor and couldn't keep Rodent company. Stressed out by the renovation, he wasn't much fun to be around anyway. The horse and dog distanced themselves from him that summer. Every morning before leaving, I lathered Misha in fly repellent and left her so that Rodent and I could drive around talking to the locals about the flood.

No one from the paper told me I couldn't take Rodent everywhere with me. In hindsight, I may have looked unprofessional, dragging my little brown dog to the sheriff's department, the water company, the FEMA office and the hospital emergency room. I'm sure Rodent did nothing to enhance my journalistic image. But everyone was still so waterlogged and in shock, nobody had the gumption or the stamina to tell me dogs were not allowed.

One afternoon I lugged her upstairs to a Rotarians' luncheon. One of the county commissioners had invited me, thinking I'd find the luncheon educational because the topic was flood disaster relief.

170

I'd never before met a Rotarian and didn't know what to expect. The meeting room was filled with conservative, well-dressed businesspeople dining on cold crab salad and artichoke hearts. As soon as the dog and I popped through the door, ninety-seven heads glared at us. Rodent and I squatted down on the floor, two steps over the threshold, trying to look invisible. I took notes. Rodent slept. We left as soon as the speakers were done.

When I interviewed the captain of the law enforcement agency, I hid Rodent under a table where she growled softly for over an hour. The captain's epaulets, his gun, his squeaky leather holster, and shiny black shoes terrified her.

I think Rodent may have been the first non-service dog ever to go inside the commissioners' office or the mayor's building. Since I refused to leave her locked up inside the hot car or have her ignored and isolated at home, she and I did all my flood interviews together.

As soon as we got home, Misha would whinny, race around the car, stick her nose in through the driver's window and cover my face with kisses. I made sure to always stop and buy a special treat for her, which I then hid in my satchel. After we'd kissed, she'd root around the car, find my bag, and grab its handle. That summer her favorite treat from the store was jellyroll cakes. I bought her at least forty of them during July and August. And while she was stuffing the cake into her mouth, Rodent was busy underneath her head, grabbing the crumbs as they fell out of Misha's mouth. When the two of them were finished, not the tiniest particle of cake was left. Misha even licked the cellophane package clean.

But even though I brought her treats, Misha was still angry with me. She despised my leaving her half the day to go do newspaper work and, to add insult to injury, Rodent got to come along with me and she didn't. She tried barricading the driveway and blocking the gate, letting me know she should not be left home alone. I wrote several more articles for the newspaper and then turned down additional assignments, using our house renovation as my excuse. I couldn't bring myself to tell my editor about Misha's acute separation anxiety and how much she needed me to stay with her.

Once I was back home (in the barn) every day, Misha stopped grazing, not because she was sick, but because she refused to leave Rodent and me. If I walked out with her and kept her company in the pasture, she'd wolf down grass until her stomach bulged and gurgled. But as soon as I headed to the barn, she was at my back. For the rest of the summer she subsisted on hay, which she munched while standing two feet outside of the barn with one eye always glued on me. If I walked to the machine shed, she followed me. If I came over to the house to check on Mark, she came too. When I went to get the mail out of the mailbox, she dashed up to the gate and waited for me. She had always been attached to me, but after my job at the newspaper, she was my shadow. Even if I wanted to, I couldn't get away.

She became overprotective of Rodent. If the dog wandered out of her sight, disappearing behind some tall grasses ten feet away, Misha would alert me by whinnying. If I didn't come out immediately to call Rodent home, Misha took it upon herself to canter over to Rodent and nudge her back. The poor dog couldn't get more than fifty feet away from the barn before Misha was hovering over her.

When the floor was nearly done, Misha began making several short trips a day over to the house to check on Mark's progress. If I was busy in the barn typing or vacuuming, Misha would dart over onto her porch and peer expectantly at Mark, who was inevitably bent over pounding nails or sawing sheets of plywood. He did not want her walking on the house floor until it was done, and I would hear him yell, "Don't you step in here, Misha, or your name is mud."

The flies hadn't invaded the barn until August, but when they did, they were brutal. My yard-long fly strips were always covered with flies. I had to hang new ones every two days. There were flies on the kitchen table, the stove, the dishes, and our bedspread. It was impossible to enjoy eating a meal because we spent so much time swatting flies. They sat on our sandwiches, the rims of our glasses, the tips of our silverware.

Misha suffered the worst, and bore the brunt of the onslaught. For eleven years, she spent her summer days on her fly-free porch or her bug-free house. When she went out to graze, I dabbed her with insect repellent and showered it off before she went to bed. But in the barn she couldn't get away from them, because the barn doors were always open. Hoards of pesky houseflies collected on her shoulders, her back, and around her eyes. She had to start wearing her fly mask inside the barn. And when I put bug spray on her, the flies swarmed onto the barn walls, waiting until she'd had her shower to land on her all over again. I couldn't leave the bug spray on her longer than twelve hours at a time because it made her skin itchy.

She put up with the flies a few more weeks and then she turned up the heat on Mark to hurry and finish the floor. She abandoned her post in the barn to stand over Mark, bringing along with her a cloud of flies. She breathed her hot breath on him so he sweated more, which caused the flies to be more attracted to him. She'd swish her tail across his head and repeatedly blow her nose over his back and shoulders. Misha had it all figured out. She knew how to pressure Mark, because two weeks later, he announced the floor was finished. "It's not perfect, but I think we are all sick of living in the barn and anxious to get moved back in."

It hurt me to watch Misha initiating my brand-new beige carpeting and glossy, knick-free linoleum. The first week we moved back in, I told Mark I thought that maybe Misha should learn to live outside. "I've never had such beautiful floor coverings. With Misha walking over it, they'll be worn and dingy by the end of the year."

I did a lot of grousing and sighing on the topic until Mark finally had enough. "I can't believe you would actually consider moving Misha to the outside just so you can keep a fancy-looking carpet. I must say, your attitude shocks me."

"Would it be so wrong of me to want a pristine house that I wouldn't have to clean every day?"

"No, it wouldn't be wrong. It just wouldn't be you. Besides, Misha couldn't survive one day outside without you. She'd commit horse suicide. She can't let you out of her sight for more than two minutes."

He was right. I was being selfish. But the first time she smeared patches of mud into my new bedroom rug, I cried. Wiping up the trail of sticky lemonade dribbles off my previously unmarred linoleum made me pound my fists into my head. Instead of screaming, though, I filled my pail with hot water and bleach and just cleaned it up. The floor looked almost as good as new. But over time, I knew it would lose its luster and go back to looking well used.

Very soon I had to decide which mattered most in the scheme of my life: new carpeting or a horse that has devoted her life to me? It was a no-brainer. I forced myself to forget how much the new rug cost and how shiny the linoleum looked when we first unrolled it. Instead, I welcomed Misha in to walk on it, and giggled when I saw how much she enjoyed it the first time she felt the thick, plush carpeting squish under her hooves.

Chapter Eighteen

I t's been over a year since we moved out of the barn
and back into our house. Misha has stomped across
our new floor hundreds of times, and it still doesn't
sag. Last Sunday I felt a summer cold coming on so Rodent and I
spent the day in bed with Misha beside us. She lay down to nap and
got up to stretch five times; the floorboards never creaked and the
joists didn't shake.

When I got out of bed to make Mark's supper, I had to force
Misha to go into her paddock. Since we've been back inside the
house, she goes for extraordinarily long stretches of time without
relieving herself. It's as if she is afraid that if she leaves me for ten
minutes, she'll miss out on something. Her bladder and intestines
have developed incredible holding powers.

Misha now has the run of the house. She's outgrown her need
to fiddle and fuss with everything and anything she finds. If she does
start wiggling her nose around a book or a plastic bag, I call her
name and she stops. She shares her treats with Rodent, and no longer
lunges after the dog's cornflakes or hash browns. My filly weanling is
all grown up, so mature that she now wanders the house without
supervision.

The years have passed in the blink of an eye. Was it really thirteen years ago that we found our worm-infested, pneumonia-laden foal? In some ways it seems like only yesterday, but in other ways it seems like a lifetime ago. I can't remember what my life was like before I had a horse living in my house.

One of the first horse books I ever read offered advice that has stuck with me all these years. The sentiment went something like this: A good horsewoman always puts the needs of her horse before her own. When she gets home from riding, she cleans her horse, she dries him off, she picks his feet, feeds and waters him, before she even considers leaving the barn to attend to her own needs. Your horse's comfort should be your number one priority.

I'd like to think that's advice I've followed. Maybe I'm deluding myself about always putting her first, but at least I know I've tried.

For the past several years, I've vacuumed my house every morning, 365 days a year. On alternate mornings, I scrub the kitchen linoleum. My windows have to be cleaned once a week because Misha loves to look out of them, steam up the glass, and drag her tongue across the pane. Dried horse saliva does not enhance a window's appearance.

Every morning, her manure must be picked up out of her paddock and heaped into a trailer. Once a month, the trailer must be emptied into the garden. In the spring and the fall when she starts to shed, I brush her once a day. From March until July she's carefully checked for ticks. She can't go outside without her fly mask and insect repellent during bug season. Nearly every summer evening, she asks to have her repellent showered off.

Misha must be exercised at least three times a week. Not short trots around the block, but miles of rigorous, aerobic cantering that increases her cardiac output and decreases her natural tendency towards restlessness. Rodent almost always comes along. When Misha gets back, her hooves are picked free of road stones before she gets a hot, cleansing shower. Next comes her reward for riding so well. I boil up a steaming bowl of brown-sugared oatmeal and pour her a big gulp of cherry or orange Kool-Aid.

She helps me cook every meal and while Mark and I eat it, she stands inches away, watching. She joins us in the bathroom when we take our baths. If the powder puff lid is not on top of the powder puff, she loves to stick her nose inside the container and blow talc all over the toilet tank.

I always keep a week's supply of Misha treats on hand. Once every two months I go to the Nickel's Thrift Bakery and fill the back of my VW Bug with day-old doughnuts and sweet rolls, and every third trip I load the front seat with loaves of bread for the fish. In late October, I make the rounds of discount stores and drugstores, looking for discounted Halloween candies. Last year a clerk gave me 146 packages of caramel corn that had been marked down to twenty cents a bag. In May, I revisit those same stores in search of discounted Easter candy. Two years ago Odd Lots sold me sixty-seven bags of jellybeans for ten cents each. Misha was allowed to eat half a bag a day, so she had jellybeans for 134 days.

Every summer, we cut three hundred bales of first-cutting hay and one hundred bales of second-cutting hay. All four hundred bales must be stored in the barn to cure; then we sell the first-cutting to local farmers in the fall. And since the best time to make hay is when the sun is at its hottest, we're usually hoisting bales when it's ninety degrees. Bits of dried grass stick to our sweaty necks and arms, poking and prodding us and lodging underneath my T-shirt. We race and hustle to beat the constant threat of rain, because ninety-degree days often bring the severest of summer thunderstorms. Once the hay gets wet, it's ruined and all our work is wasted. The only thing wet hay can be used for is garden mulch.

Once every six weeks, Mark trims Misha's hooves. Once a year, I vaccinate her and take her stool in to be checked for worms. When she's sick, I sleep out on the porch with her; when her belly is too full, which usually happens around 2 A.M., I walk her.

Having a full-time house-horse is a lifetime commitment, a little like running a dairy. Three hundred sixty-five days a year, an animal is depending on me. Every morning Misha wakes me up at 8 A.M., banging her hoof onto the metal kitchen door threshold until I let her into the kitchen. Every night at midnight, I walk with her out to the paddock and serve her supper—a bowl of corn and a big flake of hay. Seven days a week, even when I'm sick, I get up with her in the morning and go outside with her at night. In the middle of an ice storm or a power outage or suffering with my own bout of gut-wrenching intestinal flu, Misha's needs must met.

Five years ago, Misha might have spent six hours a day grazing. Two years ago, she grazed half that long. Today she grazes only when I go out with her. Our bond is wonderful and deep, but sometimes it can feel a tad constrictive.

If I had to do it all over again, would I still invite my little wean-ling to live in the house with me? Having her inside means so much vacuuming and scrubbing, so much dust and dirt. It's become almost impossible for me to leave her overnight and I feel guilty whenever I'm out shopping. I think of the thousands of day-old bakery treats I've bought and all the outdated candy I've mooched and the struggles I used to have making meals with her head inches from the stove.

Some days when I'm sick or I haven't the patience to mop the floor still one more time, I wonder if maybe I made a mistake. Without Misha in the house, Mark and I could go to restaurants, the movies, or have a picnic in the park. We'd be able to pass a bowl of potato chips back and forth between us, without having horse saliva dripping on top of our heads. I might have been a head nurse by now, with a $50,000 salary.

But when I try to imagine life without Misha always touching me, kissing me, talking to me, my mind draws a blank. For all the

178

sacrifices I've made and for everything I have given up, she has rewarded me a thousandfold. If I didn't have to exercise her, I'd probably be an obese, middle-aged couch potato. If I didn't have to vacuum every day, the house wouldn't always look so neat. If I didn't have to wake up early with Misha, I'd sleep too late and be slothful. If I still worked full-time at the hospital, I might not have discovered a new career as a freelance writer.

The older I get, the more convinced I am that life unfolds according to some prearranged plan that I really have no control over. Fate and serendipity are the bookends of my life. And the serendipitous moments in life are what I have come to savor most.

Having a horse trampling the kitchen and the living room isn't for everyone. Perhaps it's not really for anyone else but me. A healthy horse can live for forty years; that's 14,600 days of vacuuming. And when a horse spends years living in the house and it gets used to living with its owners, it would be cruel to ever push it out. Misha is a lifetime commitment.

Every once in a while I get discouraged, like when I'm not feeling well and Misha needs fifteen ticks pulled out of her tail. Or when she's left several clumps of mud on my freshly scrubbed kitchen floor just seconds after I've dumped my bleach-water pail. Sometimes I grumble and growl. But then I think to myself, "What would have happened to Misha if I hadn't adopted her? No one else would have bought her with a bloated belly and runny nose and eyes. She would have been sold for dog food." My grumbling turns to cooing, my growling into sweet talk, and I reach over and ask her for a kiss.

Adopting Misha has changed me in many fortunate and unexpected ways. And wedged in between the bookends of serendipity and fate are love, the true meaning of my life, and my purpose for living. Misha's devotion is fierce, her connection intense, her acceptance unwavering. It is as if she shares my ego, my consciousness, my being.

179

What a serendipitous gift fate has given me. I am worshipped by a horse that loves me unconditionally and believes, with all her heart, that I am a god.

About the Publisher

J. N. Townsend Publishing specializes in books about living with animals. For further information about our other animal books, please write to J. N. Townsend Publishing, Dept. CAT, 12 Greenleaf Drive, Exeter, New Hampshire 03833.

Or visit us online at www.jntownsendpublishing.com.